Awakening to Life

to Life

YOUR SACRED GUIDE TO CONSCIOUSLY CREATING
A LIFE OF PURPOSE, MAGIC, AND MIRACLES

Inspired**LIVING**
PUBLISHING

Published by Inspired Living Publishing, LLC.
P.O. Box 1149, Lakeville, MA 02347

ISBN-13: 978-0-9845006-5-9
ISBN-10: 0984500650
Library of Congress Control Number: 2018932686

www.InspiredLivingPublishing.com
(508) 265-7929

Cover and Layout Design: Brand Therapy, www.YourBrandTherapy.com
Editors: Bryna René Haynes & Rebecca van Laer, www.TheHeartofWriting.com
Photo credit. Back cover photo of Patricia: Tina K. Valant www.TinaValant.com

Printed in the United States

Dedication

To my loving husband …

My best friend, my rock, my love!

PRAISE FOR

Awakening to Life

"*Awakening to Life* will powerfully and gracefully guide you to wake up to who you truly are: a divine being full of purpose and love. Patricia weaves in her transformational journey while sharing poignant, actionable and empowering activities, strategies and new ways to uncover your greatness. She teaches you how to go to the root of suffering and replant with self-love. This is a beautiful book that will elevate your life and most definitely the consciousness of humanity."

— **Julie Reisler**, Life Designer®, author, and speaker

"Patricia Young has created an intensely valuable guidance system for people struggling with reclaiming their power and finding their true path in life. Her no-nonsense, heartfelt words offer both encouragement and support in making the transition from living a small, unfulfilling life to stepping fully into The big life we each are meant to live. Being empowered to take full responsibility for our lives is just one of the potent gifts this book offers. May you gift yourself with that empowerment and all of the other life-altering offerings within its pages."

— **Dr. Bonnie Nussbaum,** psychologist, holistic coach, and author

"Patricia Young offers clear and affirming guidance in *Awakening to Life*: Your Sacred Guide to Consciously Creating a Life of Purpose, Magic, and Miracles. Through her passionate writing and her own personal experience, Patricia shows you how to wholeheartedly embrace the possibilities of a truly inspired life, and demonstrates that you have the power to transform and consciously create a spiritually healthy life. She asks powerful questions that inspire an inner dialogue with your soul as she guides you gracefully, step by step, along your personal path to spiritual awakening. In *Awakening to Life*, Patricia gives you the spiritual blueprint for creating a life with meaning, purpose and a deep inner knowing of who you are."

— **Dr. Debra L. Reble,** Intuitive Psychologist and best-selling author of *Being Love* and *Soul-Hearted Partnership*

"Become your most authentic self! *Awakening to Life* is a fantastic guidebook for women who want to live their most satisfying, soulful and magical life. A great read for inspiration and insight on how to become your most authentic self!"

– **Shann Vander Leek,** award-winning producer, voice talent,
and best-selling author

"In *Awakening to Life*, Patricia Young shares her personal story of awakening to inspire others to wake up to the truth of who they are. Weaving her personal journey with insights and wisdom gained from her own journey of awakening and her study of Buddhism leave the reader with a rich framework for awakening."

– **Catherine Hayes,** Leadership Coach and Enneagram expert

"If you are feeling stuck, *Awakening to Life* is the key to finding the freedom to be your True Self. Patricia Young shares her personal growth through various turning points in her own life to show you how to make changes that inspire you to live your life's purpose."

– **Lisa Hutchison, LMHC,** Licensed Psychotherapist, Writing Coach for
Empaths & Artists

"Having a purposeful life really comes down to making powerful choices. *Awakening to Life* takes you through multiple exercises and beautiful, thought-provoking journal prompts so that you can tap into your internal power and bring awareness to the special gifts you possess. Patricia shares many painful and poignant turning points of her own journey that document the lessons she teaches with such passion."

– **Mal Duane,** Transformational Coach, speaker, and best-selling author

"Are you living an expansive and inspired life? We live in a challenging culture of fitting in with the status quo. In *Awakening to Life*, Patricia Young asks if we are ready to take full responsibility for our lives, so that we may experience the true authenticity we all strive for. Patricia gives us a different point of view, helping us gain a new perspective through the 'possibility' lens of life. Breaking free from the old limitations we have imposed on ourselves sets us free and opens us up to new opportunities that lead to living large."

– **Debra Oakland,** best-selling author of *Change Your Movie, Change Your Life: 7 Reel Concepts for Courageous Change*

"With little guidance to overcome the plethora of life that has covered up our soul expression, it is often difficult to find and create a life of purpose. Patricia beautifully guides those trying to reclaim the inner joy and purpose we were all born with to magically Awaken to a life of magic and miracles. A powerful message for us all!"

— **Laura P. Clark,** Master Soul Coaching® Practitioner and Trainer

"Awakening to Life is a true gift for someone undergoing a major life transition. It provides great suggestions and tips to help you reprogram your life and set intentions around where you want to be."

— **Sherry Burton Ways, ASID,** designer and best-selling author

"Awakening to Life is, without a doubt, a must-read for any woman who is ready to step into her vision and live a life aligned with her True Self. Patricia masterfully weaves her own inspiring journey of transformation into a page-turner, while providing readers with guidance for their path. Well done!"

— **Marcia Mariner,** Heart Flow Coach and business mentor

"Awakening to Life is a must-read guide that will revolutionize the way you see yourself and your purpose in life. With this book, Patricia created a powerful path for you to discover your purpose and take easy-to-implement action steps to empower you on your path. Treat yourself, and allow this book to awaken within you the power to bring purpose, magic and miracles into your life."

— **Patricia Missakian,** founder of Akashic Records Institute

"Awakening to Life is an inspiring book for anyone who's ready to live their life on her own terms. The wisdom in this book will encourage you to express more of your authentic self and say yes to your passions. A must-read for anyone who believes in infinite possibilities!"

— **Felicia Baucom,** Transformational Life Coach and best-selling author

"Patricia's heartfelt experiences shed light on what holds us back and how to discover the source within to truly live. As she steps through life lessons into a more inspired, expansive way of living, she leaves a trail for those of us interested in walking more fully in our truth."

— **Deb Coman,** content marketing strategist, copywriter, and speaker

"In her book, *Awakening to Life*, Patricia Young inspires us to step outside our limiting beliefs and to see the world of possibilities that truly lie within us. I was so moved by her honesty and courage in sharing not only great insights, but personal stories that give a glimpse into how these concepts aren't just being shared, but also were lived. If you are someone that feels like you're sitting on the sidelines of your life, this book will inspire you to jump in the game and awaken to the amazing soul that you truly are. I highly recommend this to anyone who has ever doubted their value or worth, as Patricia leaves you seeing your magnificent divinity staring right back at you."

– Shari Alyse, co-founder of The Wellness Universe, motivational speaker

"We are all on this Earth for a purpose, but many people do not know what their purpose is, or are afraid to even find out. Discovering your purpose—and then living it—is what we're destined to do. That's why I love Patricia's book, *Awakening to Life*. She helps her readers navigate these waters, allowing them to claim their purpose, and fall in love with their life as a result. Highly recommended!"

– Jill Celeste, MA, marketing coach and founder of the
Celestial Marketing Academy

"What an inspiring book filled with so much wisdom and practical guidance! Patricia's call for us to live life courageously and authentically and honor our truth and purpose in order to make the world a better place resonates so strongly with me. I love the questions to ponder and the self-nurturing practices in each chapter to consciously create a life of purpose, magic and miracles. I strongly recommend Awaken to Life!"

– Kelley Grimes, MSW, counselor, speaker, international best-selling author
and self-nurturing expert

"Love flows across these pages! 'Once we honor the part [of ourselves] that's trying to protect us, we'll start making different choices and live life by design, not by default.' I was inspired by this great quote from *Awakening to Life* by Patricia Young, a wonderful guide to awakening to take with you on your transformational journey. Written with heart, with soul, and from experience, this is the book you would recommend to your best friend."

– Anna Pereira, co-founder of The Wellness Universe

"*Awakening to Life* is both an invitation and guidebook to reclaiming our lives and creating what we really want. Patricia Young's personal stories of her own turning points are both vulnerable and inspiring. She says, 'Allowing yourself to be who you really are is your birthright.' If you are feeling called to reevaluate your life for any reason, Patricia's book can help you get started and support you to look deeply within for your own authentic answers. Awakening is a process which requires courage, truth, intention and support. This book offers journaling prompts, quotes, stories, tools and more that can help you take responsibility for loving yourself enough to live true. Learn the steps to reclaiming and committing to self-love, which Patricia says requires keeping promises to yourself. This book calls forth our confidence to truly value ourselves enough to fully embrace living an awakened and expanded life!"

— **Lynda Monk, MSW, RSW, CPCC,** Transformational Writing for Wellness
coach, best-selling author

"We are all being called to live authentically and to embrace our inner truth and power! In Patricia's empowering book, *Awakening to Life*, you will find a trail guide filled with inspiration, expert guidance, and encouragement to support you in creating a life of purpose, magic and miracles. The time to awaken to your own wisdom and power is now!"

— **Jami Hearn,** leading Intuitive Prosperity Coach, Akashic Records
practitioner and Evidential Medium

"It was a joy to read Patricia Young's *Awakening to Life*. She shares so much wisdom and inspiration on how to truly wake up and take in the fullness of the life you are meant to live. Her own powerful and courageous journey lights a path that will open the door to soul level fulfillment for so many people!"

— **Shelley Riutta, MSE, LPC,** founder and President of the Global
Association of Holistic Psychotherapy and Coaching

"On this journey we call life, it is critically important to know there are others who are sharing our path and can help us on our way. In this book, Patricia shares her story in a way that opens our eyes and hearts to what is possible and reminds us that we are not alone. Read and awaken!"

— **Camille Leon,** founder, The Holistic Chamber of Commerce

Foreword

Margaret Paul, PhD

I first met Patricia Young when she invited me to join her on one of her podcasts. During the podcast, I recognized her as a kindred soul—someone who has gone through the fire and come out the other end knowing who she is and what she wants to offer the world. It's always wonderful to connect with a like-minded person—and even more of an honor to be asked to write the Foreword for her book!

In full transparency, though, I was also a little hesitant to accept Patricia's invitation. I knew I would not be able to write the Foreword if I didn't absolutely love the book. I'm sensitive to the energy and *frequency* of a book; I only read books that have a high frequency, and in which I can feel, on a deep level, the heart and authenticity of both the book and its author. If I don't feel this, I quickly lose interest.

Awakening to Life was everything I could want in a book and more. I couldn't put the book down! I was able to not just imagine, but actually *feel* Patricia's journey toward her passion, joy, freedom and sense of purpose. I was captivated by how beautifully she writes, and how she offers inspiration by sharing her own journey and transformation in a generous and vulnerable way.

Patricia could not have written this book if she had not gone through the many challenges and dark times that she shares with us on these pages.

Her story, as well as her vision, teaches us what it means to move out of being a victim and into taking responsibility for creating—and *living*—an alive and purposeful life. She is a wonderful role model for *completely* changing her life from one of emptiness and abuse to one of aliveness, passion, integrity, purpose, joy, and manifestation.

We need as role models women who have been able to turn their lives around. It's one thing to come from privilege and always be supported in doing what your heart and soul want, but quite another to feel totally unsupported by others in following your heart and still find your way to your Divine purpose. Her journey demonstrates that this is possible for everyone—if she can do it, we all can, too!

This book beautifully explores the issues that are most dear to my heart: learning to love yourself, define your self-worth, take responsibility for yourself, connect with your higher source of love and wisdom, discover your passion and purpose, and manifest your dreams. All these things lead to living your Awakened Life—and the pathway to all of them is here in your hands.

Many blessings to you,

Margaret Paul, PhD
Co-creator of Inner Bonding, author of the upcoming book, *Diet For Divine Connection*, and best-selling author of *Do I Have To Give Up Me To Be Loved By You?*, *Healing Your Aloneness*, and *Inner Bonding*.

Table of Contents

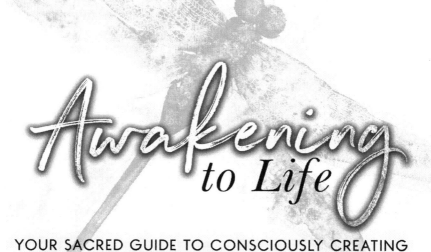

Awakening to Life

YOUR SACRED GUIDE TO CONSCIOUSLY CREATING
A LIFE OF PURPOSE, MAGIC, AND MIRACLES

Introduction

*A*re you living an awakened life?

    Maybe you don't know the answer to this question right away.

    Or maybe you're not sure, but you know you want to be more. You want to be *awake*.

As you contemplate this question, ask yourself: is your life an authentic expression of your true desires and calling? Do you allow yourself to live from the fullness of your greatness?

Although we only experience life from our own point of view, we know on some level that we're all on the same journey together; we walk side-by-side as peers as we encounter infinite opportunities. However, today's fast-paced world can make it hard to take a moment and observe where you are on your own path; it's hard to be in the reality of the present moment. We are distracted by the demands of day-to-day life and our culture. And when we go too long without reflecting on *where* we are and *who* we are, we end up disconnected from our true essence.

When we continue our journeys on autopilot, many of our experiences feature contraction, fear, confusion, and limitations. When we encounter obstacles, we just want to get by and avoid reality. When we're disconnected from who we really are, and what we really want, we experience life as a constant struggle. As we hold this belief, we restrict our capacities to be our True Selves, to share our gifts, to make love to life, and to embrace all the magic that it can offer us.

1

I believe that we are going through a transformational time on the planet, and we are all being called at a spiritual level to be part of this shift by living our lives from a more authentic place. Some of us might feel that we're at a crossroads between what we think we "should" do and what our souls have been whispering to us. I know this all too well because I was there myself for so long.

Many people are feeling the urge to connect with their life's purpose and to find ways to share their gifts and talents with the world. We all desire to make a positive impact and to live more joyful and fulfilled lives. And many of us feel a deep longing inside to do meaningful work—work that makes us feel alive and that makes a difference.

Here's the thing: it's really up to us to make our existence on this planet valuable. Nobody will do that for us; no one will come and save us. I know this because I got to a point where I had to realize that it was really up to me. There was nothing and no one coming to help, and nothing to wait for.

If you're reading this book, I'm guessing you're ready to make a change: to listen to the whisper inside of yourself. I'm here to tell you to stop waiting. Stop waiting for the day when circumstances change. Stop waiting for someone to save you. The time to claim your power is *now*. Only you are capable of changing your life in such a way that you can finally feel a true sense of freedom.

All we really have in life is the present moment. Now is the time to allow yourself to be YOU—not a new you, but the real YOU. We awaken to life when we let ourselves become who we really are— who we were created to be. In order to begin living authentic lives, we have to commit in the present moment to connecting with the truths of our hearts rather than the thoughts and anxieties in our minds.

Several years ago, I began to realize the importance of Awakening to Life. One day, after a long period of living on autopilot, just trying to get through the day, week, or year—I suddenly realized that I felt truly alive. It felt entirely different than my usual state; I wasn't bored, or anxious, or rushing to get from point A to point B. It hit me that life feels completely different in moments when you allow yourself to connect to who you really are. More, I realized that if I dared to keep choosing to live from that place over and over again, my whole experience would change. And over the past several years, it has. I decided to write this book to share how I started to connect and embody the fullness of my power, and how you can do it, too!

When I began to write this book, I had the most interesting experiences. As I sat outside to write, dragonflies flew around and landed on the rail of my balcony. Whenever I walked outside, a dragonfly flew next to me. When I drove, I sometimes saw a dragonfly right in front of my windshield. Even more oddly, I began to see a dragonfly on the screen of my kitchen window on the nineteenth floor—could they really fly that high?

My publisher and I looked at the meaning of the dragonfly and realized that it was so connected to the message of my book that the cover needed to have an image of one. Here's the meaning that we found:

> *The dragonfly, in almost every part of the world,*
> *symbolizes change and change in the perspective*
> *of self-realization; the kind of change that has its*
> *source in mental and emotional maturity and the*
> *understanding of the deeper meaning of life.*

On my own journey, I discovered that within each one of us is the power to rise above any pain or struggle; we are all capable of transforming into the highest versions of ourselves. I know this very well, as you'll see from my story. My experience with myself and my clients has confirmed to me that each of us, in our own unique way, is searching and longing for a life full of meaning. We all yearn to reconnect to who we once were, and to reclaim the inner joy and purpose that we were born with on this beautiful planet.

This book will help you become aware of who you truly are. As you read it, you will learn tools to strip off the protective layers that you built in order to navigate the world in the safest way possible. In maintaining these old habits, you may have paid a high price: you might have hidden your true essence, lost the sense of what you really want, or lost touch with the gifts that you've been given. Chapter by chapter, you will learn to reconnect with your essence and to rediscover your gifts.

Deep down, you know that there's more to life than what you've experienced so far. You want to *be* more. Maybe you've been unhappy for a while—or maybe you feel that you're outgrowing what seemed to be working well. In both cases, longing and dissatisfaction are simply signs that you're ready to come out of the cocoon you've built around yourself to keep you safe—it's become a prison. And now is the time to break free.

It's time to leave all the excuses behind and give yourself permission to discover who *you* really are and reconnect with your highest self! You need to leave who you *think* you are to the side. In this book, I'm going to walk you through a process that will help you reconnect with your soul so that you can create a daily experience of being in alignment with your true essence. Step by step, you will begin to live life with a sense of wonder, purpose, joy, and freedom, no matter what stage of life you're in. And regardless of what challenges you may be facing, *you*, my friend, are ready—the time is now. You have an important role in the world at this time.

In each chapter, I introduce practices and journaling prompts to help you connect with the principles I introduce to you in an easier way. As you journal and reflect, you will create a shift in the way you embrace life from now on.

More than anything, this book is a celebration of the miracle that it is to be alive! The planet needs more awakened people: people who are aware of their inner power, people who know who they are and what they want, and people who are ready to give their greatness to the world.

My hope is that the more of us who live fulfilled and awakened lives, the more of a positive impact we will make in the world by sharing our unique contributions, creating a ripple of goodness and love that will extend to everyone around us.

Are you ready to discover who you really are?

Let's begin together.

CHAPTER *One*

Are We Really Alive?

Are We Really Alive?

*S*o many times, I asked myself these questions:
"What does it really mean to be alive?"
"Am I really alive?"

"What about when I'm living life on autopilot, going to work every day even though I feel my job is slowly killing my soul, all because I need a paycheck and because that's what I'm 'supposed' to do?"

I used to torment myself with the question: "Is this all there is to life?" This was a very painful way of living, because I felt that I was dragging my feet every day, and I thought that if I said anything about how I was really feeling, I would be seen as a whiner. After all, who was I to question the status quo?

Here's the thing: since we left our mothers' wombs and took our first breaths, we have been considered alive … but are we really? I know that we are living beings with free will and consciousness, but are we really aware of ourselves? Aware of the miracle that is being alive? This awareness alone is breathtaking, but so many of us have taken it for granted for a long time. So, the question is: Are we really awake to our lives, to *living*—or are we just going through the motions?

Another question: What are we all about? If we don't know the answer to this, it means that we don't know ourselves at a deep level.

What do we value the most? What are our core beliefs? What are our deepest desires, our biggest fears, our strengths? What makes us *really* happy? What makes us desperately sad?

I lived for many years without knowing the answers to any of those questions. I was spiritually bankrupt. I've seen other people around me live this way as well. We tend to fill the void with material things: we accumulate possessions, and numb ourselves with food, drugs, alcohol, sex, gambling … you name it, we do it, because we don't want to face the reality.

And it breaks my heart, because I know the struggle; I know the pain and the confusion. What is even more devastating for me is to know that some people leave this planet without knowing the answers to any of those questions—without knowing what they're all about.

So, what about you? Do you go about your day, every day, unaware of how you feel? These questions may seem trivial, and maybe you're even wondering, *but what does being awake really mean to begin with?*

Well, what I have discovered, inspired by something that I once read in Wayne Dyer's book, *Excuses Begone*, is that being awakened to life is simply becoming aware of the illusion of the existence of a false self. We think that the ego, the self that has been created based on our conditioning as we were growing up, is the 'true' self. Being awakened means becoming more open and connected with your soul rather than your ego.

Being awakened to life is knowing that everything and everyone—including you—is a result of God's (or Spirit's, Source's, or Higher Power's) creation of this world. It's recognizing your own divinity, knowing that you are Spirit itself, and seeing that we're all threads of a Divine tapestry whose common theme is unconditional love. And then, it's surrender to that truth. You let yourself live by it.

As Ramana Maharshi says: "Surrender is giving oneself to the original cause of one's being. Do not delude yourself by imagining this source to be some God outside of you. One's source is within oneself. Give yourself to it."

Awakening to Life starts when you know, at a deep level, what you are all about and you *allow* yourself to become who you really are, full force. You get it: you know, deep in your heart, that you are an amazing being, and that allowing yourself to be who you really are is your birthright.

The way to get there is through unapologetic self-love. Everything else we've been taught is an illusion, and the people who we learned from were most likely not living awakened lives.

The truth is that we live in a society in which we are taught about convenience and conformism. We were not taught to connect deeply with our hearts, to follow our inner guidance, to connect with our passions and gifts, or to use them to make a difference in the world. So we end up living "practical" lives that keep us small, and don't allow us to grow and become who we really are—all because of fear.

More often than not, our parents or caregivers were themselves disconnected from their own authentic selves and passions, and were living life through the motions with so many obligations that they didn't really see our gifts and talents. Therefore, we were not encouraged to embrace our greatness from the time we were young.

A Gallup study conducted a couple of years ago concluded that over 70 percent of Americans are unhappy at their jobs. Other studies show that a great percentage of the population is unhappy in general. This means that most people are living lives that are not congruent with their authentic selves: they basically live on autopilot. They're breathing, but they're not really living. They show up at work because they need the paycheck; they stay in unhappy marriages because of the kids or for financial reasons; they put off their dreams in order to do the things that society says they "should" do. The end result is that they don't live inspired and expansive lives.

THE BIG LIE AND THE BEGINNING OF OUR SENSE OF SEPARATION

After many years of struggling, I finally realized that we were sold a Big Lie.

When we were growing up, the views and opinions of our parents, caregivers, and teachers came into play without us even realizing it. (This is true even for those of us who had nurturing childhoods.) Our culture and society had an enormous influence on us, too. Before we knew it, we found ourselves involved in this challenging and exhausting culture of "fitting in." Most of us had to obey our parents, conform to their way of doing things, and follow instructions on how to behave and please others.

So, slowly, we were conditioned and indoctrinated, and started detaching from who we really are, forgetting our innate joy and beautiful essence. It's like the real you went into hiding. That's actually where the disconnection from our soul, inner joy, and authenticity (our natural states) began.

This happened because we had no other choice: we believed and trusted our parents, caregivers, and our culture, because we thought they "knew better." We followed what we were told we "should" do, and then picked a life path that was "better" for us. I know this was the case for me, and for so many other people that I've known throughout my life.

And that way, we've been crossing off the things on the checklist that states what life should look like, and we follow the herd because "that's part of life," or because, "well, that's what everyone does." Or we're told to "get over it, because that's how it is ..." I forget how many times I heard those words; they were repeated to me whenever I had the guts to share how I truly felt.

When we look back on our lives, we see that some of the things we've done never really felt in alignment for us, but we did them anyway—because we were *supposed* to go to college, get a job, get married, buy a house, start a family, buy nice things, buy a bigger house and fancier things, etc. All this puts so much pressure on us! I'm not saying that striving for better things for ourselves is not good, but those goals need to feel authentic and expansive. They should not come from a place of "I'm supposed to" or "I should because so-and-so says so."

Somewhere along the journey, we start questioning if this is what life is all about. I know I did, so many times! But then I went back to numbing myself with shopping, exercise, sex, alcohol, and weed to bring myself "back on track," because "that's how it is." I was fortunate that I always had the strength not to fall into addiction with any of these things, but I used some of them to distract myself because I didn't have the courage to break the cycle and question the status quo.

Deep down, I knew that I had been sold a lie since I was a kid; that's why my pain and my longing were getting louder and louder as the years went by, to the point where I started getting physical symptoms.

The truth is that we were never taught to connect with ourselves, or to listen to our inner guidance and see our worthiness from within. We've mainly been programmed to look outside of ourselves, and that's how we end up shrinking to fit in and living lives that are not aligned with our own truth.

Our sense of separation starts when we believe what other people (who are themselves not living aligned to the truth of their souls) tell us what to do. By doing so, we invest years in learning to un-love ourselves. We learn to see our supposed "flaws" and to feel unworthy, and we even get to the point of thinking of and calling ourselves "broken." We learn, not to own our greatness, but to dim our light—because through the years we understand, based on what we hear and experience, that it's not safe to shine too brightly.

So we end up being one more brick in the wall, and live based on the stories that we tell ourselves about who we are, what we're capable of; why we aren't good enough, and what the future can look like for us. These stories will have a significant impact on our emotions and the actions that we'll take, which will create the life that we allow ourselves to live.

And we wonder why so many people live with low self-esteem, disconnected from their True Selves! Lacking self-compassion, they may experience anxiety, depression, and other types of illness that are so rampant in our society nowadays. It's so clear that when we go against our true natures, we feel uneasy, and we'll try to find ways to numb those emotions. The lid we're using to cover all that up will get blown away at some point!

Embracing this awareness and taking back the reins of your life is a very rewarding process, because you slowly can start giving your life shape, as if sculpting a mass of plaster or painting on a blank canvas. The final piece will contain the forms, colors, and textures that you decide to use for your creation. The final piece of that creative process is your own life—isn't that exciting?

There is so much opportunity when we embrace life and begin making our own decisions based on what feels authentic, all with an openness to infinite possibilities. No matter how dark or how lost we may feel in our current situation, that darkness can inspire new beginnings, if we're willing to embrace it, if we *consciously* choose to be open to the possibilities and not focus on our current circumstances. Like Thich Nhat Hanh says, "We have more possibilities available in each moment than we realize." We just have to be open to seeing them.

THE LIBERATING TRUTH

I firmly believe that we're going through a shift in consciousness on the planet, and it's pushing a lot of people to take part in this transformation by "being the change." Some of us can hear that inner voice calling us to live life *on purpose* more loudly than others. We're being called to live life courageously, from an authentic place, honoring our truth and our gifts, and making a difference in the world. Basically, at a spiritual level, we feel called to *awaken*. Maybe our souls have been asleep for too long, cramped in the same curled up position, trying to hide from the world, and it's time to step up and be of service—but also, to be in charge of our own lives.

For those of us that hear the inner voice loud and clear, we know that there's a point at which we can't ignore it anymore. We probably already figured out that some of the emotional and even physical struggles that we've been experiencing lately are related to "playing it safe" and putting a lid on our dreams and passions.

Some of us know that inaction will certainly bring more pain in our life. But fear and old conditioning can get in the way. At the end of the day, our biggest fear should be staying stuck and living a small life filled with self-imposed limitations. If we don't allow ourselves to grow and expand, we cannot claim our Divine right to live lives that are aligned to our values, passions, and gifts. I love this quote from Anäis Nin because she says it so beautifully: "And the day came when the risk to remain tight in a bud was more painful than the risk it took to blossom."

Each one of us, in our own unique way, is searching for a life full of meaning: we yearn to rediscover who we once were, and to reclaim the inner joy and purpose that we were born with on this beautiful planet.

I have always felt this relentless search for meaning and a life of relevance. Since I was a kid, I knew that I wanted to make a difference and to help people, but I was not sure how that would happen. As the years went by, I let fear and all that I learned while I was growing up get in the way, and I separated from that truth. But in the past few years, this longing got much stronger and louder. It was an urge that I could not ignore anymore: I feel that I have the responsibility to make my existence on this planet valuable, and to inspire others to do the same.

The truth is that what we are longing to claim today—self-love, creativity, curiosity, meaning—was so easily and naturally available when we were kids. If you don't remember, just take a look at kids. We were just like them. We were full of wonder, curiosity, astonishment, grace, and joy; we always felt whole, enough, and complete; and we never doubted ourselves for a second. We used our curiosity and creativity at its maximum potential. This was all so natural to us. We accepted ourselves the way we were and always felt joyous and free. We never thought we had to prove ourselves to feel worthy. We never thought that we would have to sacrifice who we really were, or that we would need to shrink in order to fit in. We never knew that we would need to build walls around us to protect ourselves, and we never really believed that we would have to become something other than who we came here to be just because our parents, caregivers, culture, or society said so.

The liberating truth is that it's never too late! Even if we feel at a crossroads now, we can make a choice to at least consider the possibility of changing things around to explore other options. We can get started on the path of reconnecting with who we really are.

We can connect again with our natural joy, creativity, passion, and curiosity, and listen to the wisdom of our souls to redirect our lives. The rest of our lives can be filled with joy, meaning, and a great sense of freedom. But this will happen only if we decide to do so, because, like always, we have the power of choice!

LIVING IN THE BIG LIE

When I graduated from high school, I really wanted to study journalism or psychology. I always knew I wanted to help people, and thought that, through either one of these career choices, I would be able to do so while developing my creativity. In Venezuela, where I grew up, the only option I had was to go to the city of Caracas, the capital, because the public university in my town was a mess; very often, there were riots and strikes.

One day, without my parents knowing, I drove with a friend to Caracas so that I could take an admissions test that would give me the option to be accepted into two different universities, one private and one public. While I was driving, I felt a mix of exhilaration and fear. It was a two-hour ride, and I had never driven on the highway for so long by myself, but something was giving me the courage to do this, and it felt right. It was my future ahead, and it was exciting!

I had to wait for about a month to get the results, and when I found out that I had been accepted to one of the universities, I was so thrilled and proud of myself. But when I later told my parents that I had already applied and been accepted, their reaction was not what I had expected.

We were sitting at the kitchen table when I shared what, for me, was great news. Then, I recall them asking me, "When the hell did you go to Caracas without us knowing?" Then, they told me that there was no way they would let me go to Caracas by myself. They both made it clear that they would not support me financially there. If I went, I would be totally on my own.

Thinking that I had the right answer to fix that problem, I told them that I could live with an aunt in Caracas: it would be cheaper. But that didn't go well either. My dad told me that he wouldn't put that burden and responsibility on his sister. He said, "Your aunt has two kids already. She doesn't need one more kid to worry about." He went on to tell me that I should come to terms with the idea that I was

17

not going to study in Caracas. I would find a career in my hometown, and that was the end of the discussion.

I remember feeling so frustrated, and thinking that I was being treated very unfairly. How could they deny what I wanted to do with my life? How could they make such a big decision for me, knowing that the options in Valencia were so much more limited? I went to my room and cried. I was really mad at them.

After many years, I asked my mom what the reasons behind their decision were. She told me that, from what she remembered, the university was too far from my aunt's house for me to commute there, so I would need to get an apartment in a different part of the city, and a car. They wouldn't have been able to afford it. "Besides," she said, "you were too young to be living on your own."

The thought of leaving home rather than letting my parents decide my future did cross my mind a few times. However, two main challenges kept coming to mind: I didn't have a place to stay, since I was not allowed to stay at my aunt's, and I didn't have any money to pay rent and support myself. I didn't even know where to start if I decided to leave, because I had no support. I also thought of all the suffering that I would inflict on my parents by disobeying their decision.

I could feel the weight of the guilt that I would bear if I decided to leave against their will. Truthfully, I was also very scared, because I knew I would be vulnerable as a young woman in a new and bigger city with no support. I realized I knew nothing about the big city: what areas were safe, how to move around, etc., so I was not ready to take that risk. I ultimately decided to surrender to the idea of staying at home. Doing so meant that I had everything I needed. My environment was familiar, and I felt safe. Though I was not happy with my course of study, I had a good life and had my family close to me.

Consequently, I stayed home in Valencia, and my father paid for me to attend a private university (which never made a lot of sense to me, because according to them, they couldn't support me financially in Caracas). This university had only four career choices: three types of engineering, and business administration. I reluctantly chose business administration, the least offensive of the four options to me, but not at all what I really wanted to do.

This private university also had a somewhat strict rule: students needed a minimum average on their grades to remain as students and finish their degrees. I remember that my dad bribed me by telling me that he would get me a brand-new car if my grades were above average after my first semester. I took on his challenge, thinking, "You didn't want me to go to Caracas? Fine. You'll have to buy me a car." That was the rebel in me!

It was really draining for me to take courses in accounting, finance, and math; I was never good in those subjects in high school, since my high school diploma was in humanities. Attending classes always felt like a drag, but I made a huge effort. In my first semester, I got above-average grades as well as a new car—that part was exciting! After that, it took too much out of me to go to class every day. I started failing the most difficult classes, and by the third or fourth semester, I got kicked out of the university.

I was *so* scared for my parents to find out because I knew that they would be very disappointed and mad at me. I was right! When they found out, they told me exactly that: that they were disappointed in me. They couldn't believe that they'd bought me a car and now my grades were a mess. And they resented me, because paying for school represented an effort and a sacrifice on their side. My dad didn't speak to me for about a week, and that hurt more than anything.

After a few days, they sat down with me and gave me an ultimatum. They told me that they would give me one more chance to finish my degree, or else I would need to find a job doing whatever I could. I remember crying and feeling guilty, but mad at the same time. I told them that this career had not been what I wanted from the beginning, and that it was hard for me to feel excited and motivated. They basically said, "We're sorry you feel this way, but it's up to you: either go back to school now, or get a job because you can't be at home doing nothing and having time on your hands to get in trouble."

So, guess what I did?

Yup, you're right: I finished school, and even got decent grades.

When I graduated, the next step for me was to find a job. Coincidentally, my mom knew the manager at Citibank, who told her that they were looking for personal bankers. My mom told her that I was graduating and had my Bachelor's degree in Business, so they set up an interview for me. I was twenty-three, and already feeling pretty numb from the whole career process, so I decided to give it a try. That's when I landed my first job at a bank.

Through all the years that went by, I was never satisfied with the jobs I had. I faithfully did the work that was expected of me, and I was grateful, but I couldn't get rid of the feeling of dissatisfaction and disconnection from myself. I felt I was living my life on autopilot, just going through the motions, not really living.

I dreaded every day, and lived for the weekends and time off. I would survive by drinking and smoking pot (not a lot, but enough to make me forget about the week), having sex, doing some retail therapy, or killing myself at the gym. I saw a lot of people who worked with me living in a similar way. I used to tell myself, "This can't be it. Something's missing here. There must be something else that I could do."

The first turning point in my life came in 2002 when I visited a Buddhist temple in Homestead, FL, near Miami, where I was introduced to meditation for the first time. Even though I had been reading self-help books for a few years already and had a bit of an idea about Eastern philosophy, the whole experience of being in the temple, talking to the *Ajahn* (Thai for teacher), and being taught to meditate by the monk was mind-blowing.

I went there with an open mind, not knowing what to expect: I was desperate for understanding about myself and others around me. This visit was also a way for me to find some clarity and self-actualization since I was feeling unfulfilled and very overwhelmed by so many things in my life.

Just being there felt so peaceful. The smell of the incense, the grounding energy of the place, the beautiful chants of the monks, and the beautiful statues and figures made me feel at home. While I was there, I felt that nothing else mattered.

That day opened a huge window of possibility. I was asked by the *Ajahn* to go into a small and more private area of the temple. He invited me to sit on a cushion, offered me some tea, and asked me why I was there. I told him that I felt kind of lost, and that I wanted to learn more about myself and to feel more joyful.

He started explaining the basics of Buddhism and meditation, and I started really digesting the causes of suffering for human beings: not being aware of self, not seeing the world as it is, attachment (not understanding that nothing is permanent), and desire. That's when I started understanding the concept of the ego and our conditioning. It was as if a very bright light bulb had gone off in my brain; all of a sudden, everything started to make so much more sense to me!

From then on, I started devouring books about Eastern philosophy and psychology—specifically existential and humanistic psychology. I felt an incredible hunger to learn and discover more. I felt this was really what I needed: it was like waking up to a part of me that had been put to sleep for a long time. That long sleep had created an immense amount of internal chaos, which was making me ask myself if I really wanted to continue living.

After I started going to the Buddhist temple, I reconnected with feeling passion again. That's why I was so excited about all the reading and all the learning. I relate that desperation for learning to someone who has been without food and water for a long time: all of

21

a sudden, they have access to this wealth of delicious food and drink. Reading was like that for me; I was insatiable.

In the meantime, I was still going to the temple often. The energy there made me feel so good, I felt so centered and grounded, and nothing else that was going on in my life mattered when I was there. Meanwhile, while I was going through this process of learning and meditating, I started writing a little bit. I journaled thoughts and insights, which I have included throughout this book.

Since that day in 2002 when I first set foot in the Buddhist temple, I have had many other turning points, and many big "a-ha" moments. But one of the most powerful came just a few years ago, in 2013, when two of my close friends unexpectedly passed away from cancer just two months apart from one another.

Both of these women were part of a group of friends I had known since 1993 when I got my first job at Citibank. It was devastating to know that they would no longer be here, and heartbreaking to see the kids and spouses they left behind.

During my grieving process, I dealt with so many raw emotions: shock, numbness, disbelief, anger, and a deep, deep sadness. But inside all that was a huge gift: the wake-up call I had needed for a very long time. I didn't want to look back one day and realize that I didn't have the courage to claim a fulfilling and meaningful life for myself. I didn't want to leave this world without making a difference.

I'm not sure how happy and fulfilled my two friends were before they got sick and passed on. They seemed happy on the surface, but you never know what really goes on internally for others unless they tell you. All I know is that their passing was the catalyst for me to make a huge leap in my own life, and create the work I'm sharing with you in this book. In a way, this book is their legacy.

Life is a beautiful adventure. We know when it started for us, and while we have no certainty about when it will end, everything that happens in the middle is on us. You'll learn more about my story and personal processes throughout the chapters of this book, but the truth is that in order to fully claim my life, I had to break out of the "victim" mindset that I'd settled into as a kid when I felt that my choice of education was taken from me. I had to go back to that Big Lie—the idea that there is only one way to do things "right"—and undo it in every aspect of my consciousness.

By taking responsibility for my own life and choices—even those long-ago ones—I have not only been able to find my courage, but have also been able to forgive everything and everyone I once blamed for my unhappiness, including myself. Once I allowed myself to wake up from living the Big Lie and stopped trying to hide from the world, I started creating real change in my life.

WHEN IT'S TIME TO MAKE A CHANGE

I love this quote from Sri Ramana Maharshi:

> *"Your own self-realization is the greatest service you can render the world."*

When we live in our Big Lie, we replace empowered choices with choices made out of fear. Because those choices are not aligned with our authentic self, they trap us in an endless cycle of struggle, unbalance, and unhappiness.

Sometimes, things need to happen in our lives to wake us up from the Big Lie. These events and feelings make us realize that we need to make new choices and take braver risks in order to live life on our own terms. There's a freedom that comes with this realization, and if you're reading this book, you have probably gotten a glimpse of it, and have found yourself wanting *more*. You've probably also experienced one or more turning points that prompted you to look at your life, and how you live it, in a different way.

Some common reasons for reevaluating your life include:

1. Feeling that your job provides very little meaning or purpose.

2. Getting sick and realizing that the illness or symptoms might have been created by living an unfulfilled life. (Putting a lid on our truth and dreams will create emotional and physical symptoms.)

3. Having someone close to you get sick or pass on, and questioning your own mortality.

4. Feeling constantly unappreciated and/or mistreated in a relationship, job, etc.

5. Seeing other people living bigger and fuller lives, and wondering, "Is this is all there is to my life?"

6. Wondering what the point of life is.

Living on purpose cannot wait for "someday." Someday is not on the calendar, and life is really short; we're here today, but we never know when we're leaving this beautiful planet. I became very aware of this after watching my two friends getting sick and pass away.

Here are four reasons why we can't wait for "someday":

1. *Pain and discomfort are NOT a natural part of everyday life.* We feel a lot of discomfort and dissatisfaction when we're not in alignment with our own truth and not living life on purpose—we feel a longing that gets stronger and louder, and we tend to feel out of place because we're not doing what we came here to do. That discomfort is actually giving us feedback: the stronger the discomfort, the louder the feedback we're getting. In my case, I

was experiencing frequent panic attacks at work, as well as other physical symptoms. Once I started paying attention, and took action toward living life on purpose, those panic attacks went away.

2. *Misalignment in one area can create problems in other parts of life.* Things can get very uncomfortable in other areas of our lives when we're unfulfilled. From a holistic point of view, our career can affect our relationships, our personal lives, and our health—all is connected. When we're out of alignment in one area, it will create a ripple effect in other areas of our lives as well.

3. *Joy and fulfillment are waiting for you.* There's a special kind of joy and a deep sense of fulfillment that you won't feel with anything else in your life. And here's a clue—if you can't wait to end the day, and feel drained and dragging every single morning when you wake up, you're not living life on purpose, and you're not living your Life's Purpose. We all face challenges, and we all have bad days, but if you feel a constant lack of energy and dissatisfaction, or feel drained and unhappy every day, you need to listen to the feedback and start getting clarity and taking inspired action!

4. *People need your gifts now!* I truly believe that each person was put on this earth for a unique purpose; it is as unique as a fingerprint. Not following your purpose, and not acknowledging your gifts and talents, not only dishonors who you are, and who you were created to be, but is also a disservice to those around you and to the world in general. If you don't step up, who's going to serve the people that need your unique gifts?

Awakening to your own truth and getting clarity on your passions, gifts, and what you're all about is one of the most exciting, courageous, and inspirational things you will ever do in your life. When we follow our Life's Purpose, we not only fulfill our lives, but we also start changing the world by sharing our unique contributions and creating a ripple of goodness and love that extends to everyone around us. This is what you'll learn in this book!

I know that there is an incredible loss when you don't live your life *on purpose*—your own loss of the joy of following your passions and sharing your gifts with the world, but also the loss of the people who will miss out on what you came here to share. Think about some of the people that you admire and who have made the most impact on your life. If they had not awakened their spirits and followed their hearts, you would never have known about them, and they would not have changed your life for the better.

QUESTIONS TO PONDER

I invite you to ask yourself these questions. (You can write the answers in your journal.)

- What is the Big Lie in your life?

- What made you recognize this and decide that it was time to awaken to your life?

- What would it take for you to feel filled with aliveness, vibrancy, and excitement about your life every morning?

- What are the consequences of *not* awakening to your life?

CHAPTER *Two*

Taking Responsibility for Your Life

Taking Responsibility for Your Life

Within this challenging and exhausting culture of shrinking to fit in, we are detached from who we really are and following what others believe. When I became aware of the Big Lie that touches all of our lives, I truly understood, for the first time, that the results we get in life are based on our own choices. Each one of us is responsible for our own life.

We are the gatekeepers of our thoughts, feelings, decisions, and actions. It's up to us to choose what and who we are surrounded by, what conversations we engage in, what books we read, and how we spend our free time.

It's been an ongoing process for me to become more aware of my thoughts, emotions, choices, and actions, because awareness is the key to changing anything in life. I decided that as long as I'm aware, I will no longer choose fear, stuckness, unhappiness, and constriction; instead, I choose to live my truth and to connect with my inner joy by practicing more self-love.

Do I feel fear and disappointment sometimes? Do I go back to old patterns sometimes? Of course! Everyone does at some point. However, embracing the power of awareness and the power of choice helped me find my way back to the core of my being and my deepest truth, so that I could move away from the victim role and find the courage I needed to start living life on my own terms.

A great part of the awakening process involves taking responsibility. The best way to change our lives and take complete control over them is by being responsible for our experiences, and realizing that they are the absolute result of our thoughts, our way of seeing and facing life, what we allow in our life, and the decisions that we make every moment.

We must understand that the life we have in the present moment is our own creation. There are very few exceptions: there are a few things we can't control, but we have a choice as to how we respond to those things. Yes, I know it's hard to accept this sometimes. It's easier to feel like a victim, as if life is happening *to* us instead of *for* us.

It's easier, and it feels much better, to blame someone else or our circumstances, but when we blame others or specific situations, we see ourselves as powerless and incapable of changing things in our life.

Taking responsibility means that we take our power back. When we're open to seeing the lessons, we'll be able to see the changes that we need to make. Then, we can make decisions about taking action, even if they're baby steps. Taking responsibility means that we will make new choices, not excuses. We must also be aware that if we play the victim role, that is also a choice.

Taking responsibility, being aware of what we've created and allowed, and holding ourselves accountable can be a very painful process. It requires a lot of honesty, willingness, commitment, and introspection so that we don't fall into blind spots. If you think about it, it's normal that during critical moments of emotional pain we tend to protect our "self." While we are judging and blaming others or certain situations, our ego takes control; we make excuses, and lose the objectivity to analyze ourselves and see what our options are.

We find it hard to recognize that our ego defends itself against so many negative internal conflicts and fears, as well as guilt, shame, etc. It gets carried away with feelings of "like" or "dislike" with which we have labeled past experiences. All that does is move us farther away from seeing the truth. When the mind gets clouded by these feelings, we cannot see the only truth: that we are whole, perfect, and more than enough. We are complete spiritual beings who are unquestionably loved and supported because we are part of the whole Divine tapestry.

I love this quote from Erica Jong: "You take your life in your own hands, and what happens? A terrible thing, no one to blame." I think it really captures the essence of what I was sharing above.

The good news? If we do not like what we have created or allowed up until today, we can change it! It is never too late to start having a life filled with more joy, meaning, love, abundance, peace, and freedom. We always have the power of choice available to us, and depending on how we choose to perceive life through our thoughts, decisions, and responses to circumstances, we will get different results.

Here's the thing: we'll only be able to create the results we want when we take full responsibility. We have to be open to explore our emotions, and dive deep into the root of what's causing them. We need to come from a place of curiosity, self-compassion, love, and excitement so that we can understand why we've been operating from certain patterns, why we keep taking certain actions, or why we have certain habits that are making us live a smaller life. Because underlying certain patterns and habits, there's always a payoff or positive intention that we might not be aware of. When we can understand the benefit of those behaviors, we can actually bring more compassion and love to that part of ourselves, and heal it by loving that part, understanding that it is trying to bring something positive. Once we honor the part that's trying to protect us, we'll start making different choices and live life by design, not by default.

CHOOSING FOR MYSELF

In 2002, when I went to the Buddhist temple, I had a realization: I could not continue living the way I was. Desperate to find clarity, I started reading and learning anything I could get my hands on. That decision—the choice to be open to learning a new way—was the beginning of my awakening.

The truth is that I was very unhappy in my marriage of approximately six years. He had been my high school sweetheart. I had been working at my first job at the bank for three years when we reconnected. Just as in a fairy-tale, we got married in a matter of a few months. I left everything behind in Venezuela—including my family and friends—and moved to Florida because he was living here. But after just a year or two, the fairy-tale turned into a nightmare that was breaking my heart and slowly killing my soul, making me feel numb and unable to face reality or take action.

When I first got to the United States, I could not legally work. We went through all the immigration processes, and after a year, I was given my residence and a working permit. I contacted Citibank, where I had worked in Venezuela, and after a couple of attempts I got a job.

I knew that my husband had suffered from depression before; now, he told me that he hated his job so much that he felt that he was dragging every day. He was afraid of falling into a depression again. He was very passionate about music, art, and photography, and I knew that one of his dreams was to have more time to record a CD and to work on his photography, so I told him that since I had just gotten a job, I would support both of us so that he could pursue his dreams. That way, he would feel more motivated and fulfilled. He told me that we would give it a try for a year, and if it didn't work, he would go back to a regular job.

That was the beginning of all the dysfunction. After a period of working on his music and photography, he began to show his true colors. He started losing respect for me, playing the victim role and hiding behind his depression. He blamed me for his own issues, and took neither action nor responsibility for his own life to feel better or so that we could work things out.

His music and photography didn't work out as he planned; he was not able to make a living out of it. As a matter of fact, my parents had loaned him some money for the equipment he needed, and he never paid them back. With his struggles, and only me working and providing financially, there was not a lot of money to spend, so he always felt confined and trapped, and would get to the point of blaming me for not making more money so he could do more things to distract himself.

He began to spend whole days at home, in bed. When I got back from work, he was often still in bed with all the blinds closed. I would try giving him some options for things we could do outside the house, but he would tell me that I was not sensitive enough to understand what he was going through.

I would tell him, "We have to be grateful that at least we have some options, even if they're not what you expect." Or I would ask if he could at least find a part-time job so that we could do more things. He would act like a spoiled kid sometimes, having tantrums and even getting to the point of screaming. He would tell me that I was selfish and insensitive, and that he would do whatever it took for me to understand that he was not joking about feeling depressed and not being able to work.

One of the things that scared me the most was that he had a gun. Many times, when he got into one of those tantrums, he would put the gun in his mouth and tell me that if I said anything else he would pull the trigger; it would be my fault, and my responsibility to clean up the mess. I remember running down the stairs crying and covering my ears, hiding in the half-bathroom we had downstairs, and begging God not to let him do anything stupid.

Another way in which he would demonstrate that he was not joking about his depression was by scratching his own arm in front

33

of me to show me how I made him do messed up things because I was not being sensitive, or I was saying too much or too little.

After a few of these disturbing events, I told him that he needed to see a psychiatrist, and he agreed. He started taking medication and going to therapy. Still, he would stop the medication, or mix it with alcohol. He would skip his sessions, claiming that he didn't like the therapist. Even after he switched to a new therapist, he made the same excuses to stop going.

He even took himself to the hospital a couple of times, only to call me the first night begging me to get him out of there. He once blamed me for making him want to go to the hospital. There was no consistency or taking responsibility on his side.

I was on a continuous emotional roller coaster. That really started getting to me, because I felt that I had no life. I spent my whole work day worrying about what solutions I could suggest when I came back home, hoping that he would feel motivated or be in a better mood than he had been when I left. I had no friends, and if I wanted to do something for myself after work, he would criticize me and tell me that I was selfish because he had been home alone the whole day.

No matter what I said, did, or suggested, in his opinion, I was never sensitive enough to understand what he was going through. According to him, I always thought I knew everything, or that I had everything figured out.

The emotional/psychological abuse on his part progressively escalated until, near the end of the marriage, it turned physical. He never really beat me up, but he did slap me a couple of times. I'll never forget the last time he hit me: I got a bruise on one side of my nose, and when he saw it the next morning he said, "Please cover that up with make-up. I can't believe you made me do that to you." That's when I really saw it clearly and said to myself, *I need to get out of this marriage!*

I'm not saying that we didn't have beautiful experiences; we had a lot of them, but his dark side was very dark, and towards the end of the marriage, there was a lot more of the darkness. I tried so many things to help him feel happier and more fulfilled, thinking that if he was happier, I would be happy again, too. But nothing seemed to work.

At the end of the day, it doesn't matter how dark we feel our lives are: each one of us is responsible for making decisions and taking actions to make things better. I couldn't help him if he was not willing to help himself. But at the time, I didn't understand this. I actually got to the point of believing that our issues were my fault, just as he said they were. I felt that there was something wrong with me, that I was broken. *How can I live with myself,* I thought, *if the man that I love the most is miserable because of me?*

I remember parking my car at work one day on the eighth floor of the parking lot. There were big openings on the walls, like windows. I stood near the edge and stared down to the floor. For a moment, I felt that was the solution to all of the pain and feelings of failure was simply to let go and fall. "Do it Patricia," I said to myself. "It's so easy. Jump, and all the pain and shame will be cleared away."

What made me stop in my tracks was seeing something like a picture of my family in front of me: I could see their faces, and I started crying, overwhelmed with shame that I would even consider something like this. My parents would be devastated, my sister, my nieces … they didn't deserve to go through that pain! I saw it very clearly: my husband was the one with issues, not me. He was not worth my family's suffering.

But I needed clarity on so much else. So I started therapy for myself. That, plus what I was learning in the Buddhist temple, helped me see that we are all responsible for our own lives, choices, and actions. After a lot of resistance, I came to the realization that my best bet was to get a divorce, because things were not going to get better. I couldn't make my husband choose to stop playing the victim and take responsibility for his own life, but I could make that choice for myself.

The thought of getting a divorce was devastating because I had the example of my parents, friends, and other family members who were married for life. Going against that example of "what should be" was very draining and overwhelming. At the same time, I was laid off from my job at the bank in Miami, and this added more stress to the whole situation.

My parents were in Florida because they were selling a townhouse they owned as part of their preparations for leaving Venezuela and going back to Spain, where they both had been born. When they saw me, they knew something was going on. I was really thin, and looked haggard. The stress was taking its toll.

I opened up to them and told them that I was very unhappy. I didn't share all the details with them, but they understood that there was abuse involved, and we agreed that I would move out while they were here, because we all were afraid of what he might do with his gun. They also encouraged me to come to Spain with them and start fresh in a new place, and I agreed.

I remember the day I left. The night before, he had been drinking, and he and my dad had a big argument. He had disrespected my mom during a conversation, and my dad could not contain himself; he started telling my husband how he felt about him. Out of desperation and fear, I ended up telling my husband that we needed to go home. In the car, he yelled at me for not standing up for him, not defending him in front of my dad, and all I said was that I didn't want to talk about it because he had disrespected my mother.

When I woke up the next morning, it was a Saturday. I told him that I wanted to go spend the day with my parents because they were leaving for Spain soon. He started yelling at me again, telling me I was selfish and that he could not believe how low I had sunk. I felt that if I didn't speak up, my heart and my throat would explode.

I knew that he had the gun in our room, but I couldn't take it anymore. I ended up screaming at him, telling him that I was done with him and his abuse, that I was miserable, that this marriage was killing me and I wanted a divorce.

After saying my piece, I rushed to the closet and shoved a few things into a bag really quickly. He was screaming, asking "How could you do this to me? You think you're always right, but you're making the biggest mistake of your life. No one will love you like I do!"

When I came out of the closet and he saw me with the bag, he threw his wedding ring at me.

I ran downstairs, because I was not sure if he would pull out the gun and try to manipulate me like he had done so many times before. I made it to the car and started driving, trying to catch my breath. I called a friend we had in common, who knew a lot of what was going on, and told him what happened so he could check on my husband. I didn't want him to do something stupid. I also called my parents to tell them what had happened and that I was on my way to them.

When I got on the highway, I had to pull over, because I was really sobbing and literally felt like my heart was breaking. I had such a pain in my chest, I felt I couldn't breathe … I was leaving the person I thought was the love of my life behind. It was over, that chaotic chapter of my life to which I had held on for so long, thinking that it could be fixed. It was finally over. I didn't know what my life would look like from then on, but somewhere deep inside, I knew this was the right step. I felt inexplicably supported by the Divine.

On Monday, I talked to a divorce attorney that a friend recommended, and started the divorce process. I looked for a temp job close to my parent's home, and I stayed with them until they sold the townhouse, which took around three weeks or so. Of course, my ex tried to make my life miserable in the meantime, calling me and manipulating me, telling me that he was hospitalized because he was thinking of taking his own life. He left very nasty messages on my cell phone if I didn't answer; after I changed my number, he left them on my parent's voicemail. At least I had my parents' support, and my sister had flown in too, so that helped a lot.

When my parents left for Spain, I stayed at a friend's house until the divorce was finalized and I was able to put things in order. Then,

37

I got on a plane—and, just like that, left everything behind to start a new life in Spain. I was so numb that I had no idea how I really felt about it all, or what being in a new place would look like.

This was one of the most challenging and painful times that I have experienced in my life: being laid off, finally deciding to leave my husband after seven years of marriage, and moving to a new country—all within six months—took an emotional toll on me. However, taking responsibility and making the choice to leave that dysfunctional relationship opened up a whole new dimension of self-discovery, self-awareness, forgiveness, and self-love in my life.

Again, sometimes big things need to happen in our lives to wake us up and make us realize that we need to make new choices, take braver risks, and experience freedom. At the end of the day, we are always creating with our decisions and what we allow in our life.

THE MAGIC THAT HAPPENS WHEN WE TAKE FULL RESPONSIBILITY

Once we make the brave choice to start taking responsibility, we will start noticing amazing changes in our lives. Here are some of the rewards that you may experience:

1. *You will feel a sense of accomplishment.* You'll feel empowered, discover a new sense of self-respect, and cultivate your self-esteem.

2. *You will experience real growth and expansion.* You'll be making decisions for yourself, and writing your own story. Infinite possibilities lie ahead.

3. *You will step away from dependency (or codependency).* The only person you count on at the end of the day is you: you're your life partner. Yes, you can get support from others, but once you start taking more responsibility for your own life, you'll begin to set healthy boundaries and make decisions that will take you closer to your own goals and dreams. YOU are in charge!

4. *You'll become a master at manifesting.* You're the one making the choices, so you can identify things that you want or need, and get clear on what you will and will not allow in your life. Taking action will start to feel more natural, because you'll see that aligned actions create the results you want.

5. *You'll feel more in control of your life, and give yourself permission to live a life that feels more authentic.* You'll no longer blame others or your circumstances. You'll no longer have the sense that you want to escape from your own life. And, you'll start feeling that you deserve more in life, so you'll do what feels right more consistently.

WHY SOME PEOPLE AVOID RESPONSIBILITY

Why do so many people avoid taking responsibility in their lives?

There are many reasons—but mostly, they fear the unknown, and fear they don't have what it takes to create a life that feels more authentic. They may understand that they need to make a change, but lack the clarity they need to start taking action, and fear making the wrong decision. They fear that, if they began to make changes, they will lose people or things in the process. They fear what people will think or say about them.

39

The common thread is *fear*.

Fear of judgment can really keep us stuck in very uncomfortable situations, be it relationships, jobs, etc. Fear held me back for a long time. I feared what would happen if I disobeyed my parents and went to Caracas for college, so I let go of my dreams to pursue a business degree. I feared that everyone would judge me or stop loving me if I got a divorce (because, in my family and our social circle, everyone was married for life), so I stayed in a dysfunctional relationship for far too long.

I can tell you, from my own experience—and from what I've seen in the lives of my clients and other people close to me—not taking responsibility for ourselves can lead to:

- Stagnation

- Feeling that life is a constant struggle

- Boredom

- Looking for coping mechanisms to fill the void (self-destructive habits and addictions)

- Anxiety

- Feeling hopeless, depressed, and even suicidal

If we don't really take our power back and take responsibility for our own lives, we will not grow. Instead, we will remain stuck in our old patterns, our same struggles, getting the same results over and over again but still hoping for something different—a behavior which matches Einstein's definition of insanity.

So, we have to remind ourselves that we are the creators of our circumstances. We are responsible for our own choices, for what we allow in our life, and for the results we get. We are responsible for the quality of our lives—nobody else is.

THE GIFT OF STRUGGLE

With a lot of practice, I have found that in moments of deep and intense struggle in my life, the secret for me to come out on the other side stronger and wiser has been to really connect with my feelings, and to surrender myself to the truth that we're all part of a Divine tapestry that is made of unconditional love and which supports me at all times. No matter what I see in my present circumstances, Divine love is always there for me.

I remind myself that struggles are nothing more than a great opportunity to experience growth, align to my higher power or greater source, allow for grace, and trust that everything is working out for the highest good of my soul. Basically, I've had to learn to let myself surrender, and to live through that highest part of myself.

I have learned the hard way that we are not able to solve any challenges, situations, or struggles at the level at which they were created. We need a new awareness, a new level of consciousness, to see our situations or struggles from a different point of view; then, we can see the possibilities.

I have had to be reminded *many times* that struggles, when I'm open to receiving the lesson, allow me to heal and break free from old limitations that I have imposed on myself and from agreements that I have made in the past. These show up as limiting beliefs, thought patterns, habits, and attitudes that are no longer serving me—and that, in fact, are actually keeping me spinning my wheels and living small.

I have been learning that my soul's struggles—if I'm open to seeing them as opportunities—are invitations to take down every wall I put up around my heart, and to reconnect with every part of myself that I shot down while I was growing up. When I do this, I can deepen my connection with myself and the Divine, grow and evolve, and pave the way to understanding other people's struggles so that I can be of better service on the planet.

41

If you really think about it, we struggle because we are trying to prove, whether to ourselves or others, that we are worthy and lovable. But the more we try to prove this, the further away we get from believing in our own worth and seeing that we are unconditionally loved by the Divine for no reason other than that we exist.

If we're not aware of this, we can get caught up in a painful cycle. When we try to validate an external change that we can't seem to make within, it makes it so easy for our brains to find evidence that we're not supported and that our life is a struggle. We let doubt creep in and give in to a deeper sense of separation, as if it's the world against us, and we're alone fighting this tedious battle called life every day. I know I felt this way for a very long time, resisting the lessons and feeling alone in the process—and it was so exhausting!

So, I have had to learn to surrender to the idea that most of the time, what we feel as a struggle is in Divine order, and has a meaning, because the Divine works it out for us. It will direct us to have the experiences that will teach us the lessons we are meant to learn, release the blockages that need to be released, or even create something that someone else needs.

We are all supported by the Divine, and we are all connected—we are one. By being in flow with life, we get out of our own way, and allow ourselves to see the synchronicities and opportunities that will lead us to follow our vision and purpose, if we're open to seeing it.

This isn't always easy. When we intentionally choose to live at a higher vibration, everything that is not of that vibration will come to the surface so we can heal it, clear it, and turn it into a higher vibration. This will feel uncomfortable; it will feel like struggle. But if we choose to stay with it, it will become part of our transformation, just as the caterpillar transforms into a gorgeous butterfly

So, the best way to move forward when we are struggling is to embrace it, and to understand and trust that it is part of our growth process. One of the first things that we can do is to acknowledge the fear or the anxiety that this awareness generates. Don't resist it: simply acknowledge it and feel gratitude for it, because it's a signal of Divine expansion knocking on your door.

Keep in mind that it's all about perspective, so get excited. The struggle is trying to teach you something that will move you forward, and from a place of compassion and curiosity, you will find out what core belief is underneath.

I've been surprised to see that, for me, it's usually a perceived experience where I've contracted myself and gone into fear or felt inadequate over something that didn't let me see the bigger picture. It's as if I went into my default limiting beliefs and immediately closed down without allowing myself to see the whole situation. I just saw what my level of self-awareness allowed me to at that time.

I like to say that we just need to stay in the room with it, and approach it with curiosity. Even though it feels uncomfortable, we need to be aware that this is the work of clearing the mental and emotional clutter, and it's part of the growth process, so get excited! The more we release, the more we'll start experiencing more soulful experiences.

As we clear and heal layers of fear and limiting beliefs, we give up conflict and struggle, and we can take our mind out of the way of our soul's beautiful path, so we grow and expand into higher versions of ourselves, stop feeling that sense of separation, and tune in to the wholeness that is our Divine nature. And this, my beautiful friends, is one of the greatest gifts found in struggle.

For me, the process of starting to live a more awakened life started when I began to allow myself to navigate my feelings with more ease and grace, and from a place of curiosity and compassion. That has helped me enjoy more every single moment, every single part of my process: I laugh more, love more, am more authentic, tap more into my creativity, am more curious, forgive more, am kinder, feel more freedom, do more of what I love, and repeat non-stop.

The whole point is that we need to enjoy the simple fact of being alive—smile at life every time we see a sunrise or a sunset, the beauty of a flower, the innocence of a child, or the unconditional love of a pet. Smile when we hear the music of a bird chirping, and love our essence reflected in our fellow humans when we witness acts of random kindness for others.

Living is not only becoming aware of the spark of life that exists within us and in those around us, but is also being aware of the source of life that feeds our soul with every single breath that we take. We take so many things for granted, but really, being alive is such a beautiful and magical miracle!

We need to embrace life from that magical place. It is so amazing how we can get off track so easily if we don't remain mindful and aware. We let outside distractions, past habits, and old thought patterns take over our authentic selves, and then our egos take control of the steering wheel while we navigate through life. We can't dismiss our spiritual nature and replace it with a false sense of self and separation; this only brings struggle and suffering in life.

We really need to be aware that we're part of a higher consciousness, and the way to connect to it is by using the power of our thoughts to maintain that unity with the Divine. Otherwise, we create separation—we will feel that our "selves" are cut off from the Divine. Again, it's as if the whole Universe is against us, and when we do that, we inevitably suffer and live life from a place of fear, lack, and limitations, usually seeing ourselves as something separate from the Divine tapestry and as victims, because we're disconnected from that great source of Universal love.

QUESTIONS TO PONDER

- What is the biggest challenge you are currently facing in your life?

- How do you think you're creating this challenge (or allowing it to happen)?

- What do you think is the payoff or positive intention behind it, when you allow it or don't change it?

- What would you like to experience instead?

- What actions can you start taking to change things around (even if it's a baby step)?

CHAPTER *Three*

Loving Yourself
Into Freedom

Loving Yourself Into Freedom

*W*hen we view ourselves through the blurry lens of the ego mind, we see a distorted image of ourselves: our flaws and imperfections are magnified. Our ego mind is a collection of concepts that we have attached to; from them, we create our self-images. Then, we go on to invent self-stories: beliefs about who we are and what we're capable of, based on our self-images. Our self-stories drive the decisions we make and the actions we take, resulting in the experiences we live. Those experiences in turn confirm what we already believe to be true about ourselves.

In Chapter One, I described how, as we grew up, we found ourselves involved in the challenging and exhausting culture of fitting in. Slowly, we started detaching from who we really are, forgetting about our innate joy and beautiful essence. A big part of this process is the creation of self-stories that emphasize our flaws and distort our True Selves.

We invested years in learning to un-love ourselves; we learned to see our supposed flaws. We began to feel unworthy, and even got to the point of thinking of ourselves as "broken." We learned not to own our greatness; we dimmed our lights, because based on our experiences, we created self-stories that have been running our lives and keeping us stuck.

When you don't love yourself, you may feel that you're in a suffocating prison—one that you for yourself. I've been trapped in that prison, too. Once inside, we continually seek an escape by looking outside of ourselves instead of looking inwards. This makes the whole cycle even more painful.

As long as we continue to base our lives on old self-stories, we will feel unworthy and broken. When we don't own our innate greatness, we become more distant from the possibility of self-love and connection with our real self-worth.

So how do you escape the prison that your ego mind creates—the prison of your limiting self-story?

Here's the thing: we don't have to fight our ego mind. We just need to understand it. Our ego mind takes its main job very seriously: it attempts to "protect" us. When we understand that and see it from a place of curiosity and excitement rather than judgment, we become more aware of it. With this clarity, we empower ourselves to make new choices, to change our stories, and to live life with more freedom.

The more we understand how we operate, the more we will be receptive to our own divinity.

Our self-love immediately increases when we stop identifying with the false beliefs we've developed throughout the years. We begin to see and experience who we really are: *beautiful, spiritual beings who are whole, perfect, and complete.*

We all have to take responsibility for knowing who we really are and for acknowledging our beautiful essence by understanding these simple facts:

1. Our self-worth should not be based on approval or validation from others, or else we'll end up as "people pleasers" and/or doormats.

2. Our self-worth is not based on things that we gather from outside of ourselves, the material things that we own, or the size of our bank accounts.

3. Our self-worth should not be based on how we look. We need to love ourselves from the inside out and be grateful for the miracle of our bodies and our senses.

4. The worth of our True Self is intact—nothing can change it, and nothing we do can take that away from us.

5. The greatness, amazing light, and beauty that we see in other people is within us too; it's a reflection of who we are.

6. When we center our self-worth on performance or results, our self-worth will fluctuate based on the outcome and will not be based on our innate beauty.

One thing is for sure: our lack of self-love has shaped our perspectives and decisions. Many of us get so caught up in the roles we play every day that we lose sight of who we really are. We end up living on autopilot, and many of our decisions are fear-based; we tend to settle for less than we really deserve in our careers, relationships, and more.

Self-love means letting go of the need to be what others want us to be.* Instead, we must unapologetically allow ourselves to bloom into who we came here to be. When we love ourselves the way we are right in this moment, we empower ourselves to live lives filled with more joy, meaning, love, abundance, and freedom.

So keep this in mind, today and every day: you are responsible for giving yourself love. Always acknowledge and appreciate your own worth. It's also true that when you love yourself, you open yourself to love from others as well.

*As a gift to you, I invite you to download my free Self-Love meditation to release layers of beliefs that no longer serve you, and to create the space for renewed energy that will allow you to grow and nurture your self-worth. Download it here: www.InnerProsperityAcademy.com/self-love-confidence-meditation

QUESTIONS TO PONDER

1. Where do you feel you don't love yourself or that you're unworthy?

2. Where and how could you be projecting this lack of self-love onto others, thus adding to the painful cycle?

3. Where do you prevent yourself from experiencing freedom by making choices based on old stories?

When we truly value ourselves and possess high self-worth, we participate fully in our own lives without settling for less, without shrinking to fit in, and without judging ourselves or others. We live our lives on our own terms.

THE HEALING BEGINS

In Chapter Two, I told you the story of my divorce. As you know, my parents had planned a move back to Spain; they wanted to leave Venezuela and the camouflaged dictatorship that had emerged there. They suggested I come to Spain with them and start fresh. That way, my ex-husband couldn't search for me, manipulate me, or make me miserable again.

It was a very tough decision. I had already lost my job and ended my marriage; if I moved, I would also leave my life in the U.S. behind. I would have to start from scratch in a different country. The prospect was overwhelming. I felt so numb that it was very hard to think clearly and make decisions.

After a lot of consideration, I finally decided to make the move. I planned to stay with my parents for a few months until I could think more lucidly.

While I waited for the legal papers I needed to work, I began to heal. I slowly started going back to the gym. I began to research holistic modalities; I wanted to find treatments that would help me to recover emotionally and physically. I was always exhausted, and I knew that I was depressed. However, I didn't want to go to a regular doctor. I knew they would prescribe antidepressants, and I didn't want to go that route.

During this period, I took time to think about what I had always wanted to do. I brainstormed activities I believed would feed my soul, but that I hadn't given myself the chance to try while I was married. I made a list of them and did some online research on each one.

I took some beginner's music and vocal classes. I kept meditating, and I looked for wellness centers. Soon, I found out about Reiki. I got a few sessions done, and I fell in love with it. I experienced so much healing—physical, emotional, spiritual—after each session that it blew my mind. I decided to enroll in a class, and I became a Level 1 Reiki healer.

After about six months with my parents in Valencia, I got my legal documents in order. I was no longer so depressed and numb, so I decided to move to a town that was very close to Barcelona. I had visited the city on a quick trip and fallen in love. It was quite expensive, so the suburbs were a more practical choice.

I found a job as the office manager for a small local company, which would allow me to support myself while I continued my healing journey.

A very supportive friend suggested that I started painting as a therapeutic practice. At the beginning, I was very resistant to the idea, because I had never painted before. Although I was willing to try new things, I had never believed that I was creative. Despite my doubts, he got me some brushes and acrylic paint. At first, I started painting on regular paper. To my surprise, I enjoyed the process, so I decided to try small canvases. Soon, I discovered that painting abstracts and using mixed media became a great way to release the

53

crap that was entangled inside of me.

Painting changed my life completely. I spent real, intimate time with myself. While I painted, I submerged in another world: I could feel that I was getting deeply and purely in contact with my center. I listened to my soul and to the things it had to say; I felt my emotions. I painted them all onto the canvas—the only language I had to express them back then.

I have continued to paint, and even now, it is a spiritual experience: a way of knowing myself more deeply, and a way in which I allow myself to freely play and tap into my creativity. When I paint, I grow.

I had to quit my job as a sales rep after only a few months because my boss sexually harassed me. Painting helped me work through that experience, too. Soon, I found another job as a sales rep for a company that sold training conferences to big companies, and this job was in Barcelona City: there was another move on the horizon.

Although the city was closer to my job, rent was more expensive there. I moved into a shared apartment with two roommates. This was an experience I had never had, and it was interesting to share space with two different personalities. One of them was a jazz singer, very talented and creative, which inspired me to keep tapping into my creativity. The other was a college student who was finishing his degree in engineering.

In Barcelona, I found a Tibetan Buddhist Temple that I went to often, as well as a place with Reiki healing circles. In a matter of a year or two, I was in a much better place emotionally and spiritually. After a long time, I had connected with my heart again. With my new clarity, I decided to pursue Level 2 Reiki certification, and take a Massage Therapy certification course as well.

All these classes taught me that, deep in my heart, I wanted to serve others. However, I never believed that I would be able to support myself financially doing Reiki and massage. I continued working corporate jobs while doing what I really loved on the side.

It was only after I began to love myself more fully that I could even imagine making my passion my work, and it took me years to get there. Now, though, I can see that what felt once like my biggest heartbreak was just the beginning of my reconnection to my heart at a deeper level. I came to understand that my ex-husband did not break my heart with all that he did. What he broke were my expectations.

All my experiences in the aftermath of my divorce have helped me to get closer to my heart, and to love myself in a bigger and more beautiful way. I allowed myself to unapologetically explore what I really wanted; now, I know that this process was what my soul really needed to evolve and become who I am today. Otherwise, you wouldn't be holding this book in your hands.

The main key to self-love is to allow ourselves to be in the process, and to be open to seeing the lessons which bring growth, expansion, and freedom.

RECLAIMING SELF-LOVE

To reconnect with our self-love, we need to cultivate the space to find ourselves. We must honor where we are, have compassion for ourselves, and avoid judgment and comparisons to others. When I got to Spain, I accepted where I was—pain, fear, and all—and that was the beginning of my beautiful self-discovery journey.

As you reclaim your self-love, it is important to become aware of your daily commitments. Have you checked in on how well you're keeping commitments to yourself lately? This requires giving yourself the time and space to disconnect from everything so that you can turn your attention inwards and really listen.

You're probably *interested* in achieving your goals, and in living a life that is in alignment with your values, passions, and gifts. But are you *committed* to living your life *on purpose*? There is a huge difference between being *interested* and being *committed*.

Are you clear on what you are committing to every day? Because here's the thing: we're always committing to *something*, whether we're conscious of it or not. Self-love requires that we keep promises to ourselves. If you're not committed to self-love, you may find yourself unconsciously committed to your old self-story.

Think about it: it's hard to stay confident when we keep breaking promises to ourselves. More, how can others have confidence in us if we don't trust ourselves?

For me, it took commitment to embrace self-love. I started by getting clear on what my promises were, and then I decided what was negotiable and what was not from that moment on. Finally, I was able to keep my promises. When I trusted myself, I made more and more room to explore my soul's needs.

To start committing to self-love, we have to get very clear and establish what is non-negotiable in our personal lives and in our careers. Then, we can decide what *is* negotiable. When we are clear with ourselves, it makes it easier to be consistent, to have healthy boundaries in place, and to have brave conversations with other people as well. The key is to be decisive and to stop making exceptions. Then, we can steadily keep those promises to ourselves.

To make it easier for you, here are my "5 Steps for Keeping Promises to Yourself" so you can nurture your self-love and grow your self-trust muscle.

5 Steps for Keeping Promises to Yourself

1. *Create sacred space.* Sit in silence for a few minutes and connect with yourself, preferably in a space that you find relaxing. Give yourself permission to get the clarity you need about what is non-negotiable and what is negotiable in all areas of your life (personal life, career, etc.).

2. *Write your promises down.* There's a special kind ᴏ. magic when you write down your promises to yourself. Be specific, but keep it simple. You can start with small promises so that you can start to collect evidence and to build your self-trust. You may want to use a beautiful journal that inspires you.

3. *Revisit your journal daily.* Energetically connect with your promises by reading them every morning and evening. You can also keep your promises visible on post-it notes, or set up reminders on your phone during the day.

4. *Keep track of your progress.* Journal about your progress. Reflect on your wins and your challenges. Think about what you are doing well, and what you need to continue to improve. Remember: there are never mistakes, just learning experiences. Mistakes are only "Missed-takes," and you always have more takes ahead, and the opportunity to course-correct!

5. *Celebrate yourself!* Following through gives you satisfaction and a sense of great achievement. It also raises your trust and confidence in yourself. Make sure you honor yourself by doing something special to celebrate you!

QUESTIONS TO PONDER

•   Are you *interested* or *committed* when it comes to reclaiming your self-love? What would be a sign that you're actually committed?

- Where in your life are you committed to growth?

- How are you getting to know yourself at a deeper level?

- Where can you honor your truth and make a difference?

- Where in your life do you feel you are hiding behind your routines and fears? Are you playing small because it's safer that way?

FINDING BALANCE

To help you keep your commitments, you also need to find more balance. A well-balanced life is essential for our general well-being and happiness. Even though the results we get in life are mainly based on our thoughts, emotions, and actions, we can't plan, control or anticipate everything that happens in our lives. However, we *can* always choose how we'll respond and how we'll use our energy.

When it comes to balance, what works for some people does not necessarily work for others. This means that you have to check in with yourself and be aware of what it means to you to be balanced. How do *you* know you're living in balance? What does it feel like when you're in that "sweet spot"?

We need to make sure both our external and internal lives are in balance. When your external life takes on more focus, you may find yourself pushing yourself at work, attending a lot of social events, doing a lot of things that are fun, or attending to your family's needs. When this happens, you may be paying less attention to what's going on inside of you. You may lack the time to rest, to set healthy boundaries, or to practice self-care.

On the other hand, if you spend too much time in the internal space of self-reflection, pushing yourself intellectually, having a rigid routine of self-care, etc., you could be missing out on the experience of living, spending time with your loved ones, and having fun.

Everybody feels balance in a different way, but when you get awareness of what it feels like to be out of balance, you can recognize it faster. Then, you can reframe it, go inward, and become aware of what needs to be done. At the end of the day, the discomfort that is generated by being out of balance is simply your awareness that you are feeling separation from the Universal tapestry that you're part of.

QUESTIONS TO PONDER

- What are some emotional clues that tell you you're out of balance?

- Where do you feel unbalanced in your body?

- What causes you to fall out of balance?

A MORE CONFIDENT YOU!

Self-confidence is one of the keys to our happiness and success—and yet, I see a lot of people struggle with this issue every day. Believe me, I've been there, too! Self-confidence is a mental state and a skill. It can be developed and cultivated if we make the *conscious choice*. I like to think that when we're confident, we're in harmony with the Universe!

When we don't have confidence, nothing else matters. Many people link their self-worth to approval and validation from others, to material things, or to the outcomes of certain events. Then, to feel better, they try to change their bodies, the way they look, or the way they dress—but they're not making the real shifts that could change their lives. Some people have everything in life: money, success, looks, and even fame, but deep inside they still lack a real sense of confidence and worthiness. So how do we make changes that count?

We all come to the planet loaded with confidence and a great sense of worthiness. You only have to take a look at kids around you to see that they are confident, creative, and spontaneous; they know they're enough, and they don't doubt it for a second.

The truth is that we don't lose that gift: it just gets dipped under layers of limiting beliefs and shAme that we collect as we grow up (this is not a great collection to have!). As I discussed in previous chapters, we're encouraged to fit in by the people we meet, and by our culture. As we try to conform, we develop distorted images of ourselves. Those images reflect and magnify our perceived flaws and imperfections, not our True Selves.

As a result of these distorted images, we tend to limit our potential—to the point that we often feel that we don't deserve good things. We don't let abundance, success, and love into our lives.

One of the greatest reasons people live with limitations is self-judgment. As I told you at the beginning of this chapter, the beliefs that we have gathered throughout the years create our self-images and drive the actions we take, resulting in the experiences we live.

When we have a limited sense of self-worth, we can't see the limitless possibilities that lie ahead of us. Instead, we put lids on our expectations; we shrink away and suppress our desires. We let ourselves believe that we're not worthy of good things—health, money, relationships, and a fulfilling life. We find ourselves in those prisons of our own making.

Here's the key, though: when it comes to confidence, we *only* have to look within. What keeps us from seeing this simple truth? We live in a very visual culture, so we spend a lot of time thinking about the outside. But our confidence is not found outside; it only exists within. We just have to learn how to reconnect with it and nurture it.

There's a very simple formula: low confidence is directly linked to how we feel about ourselves, and the inverse is also true. High confidence is directly linked to a positive self-image.

Confidence has a tremendous ripple effect. How you feel about yourself directly impacts the decisions you make. I once read something in *A Course in Miracles* that I recognized as so true it felt like a stab:

Every decision you make stems from what you think you are, and represents the value that you put upon yourself.

How we feel about ourselves shapes what we tell ourselves, as well as our thoughts about ourselves. The stories that we tell ourselves every day can create positive or negative feelings that result in our high or low confidence.

The most common story that we tell ourselves is that we're not enough. I've been there myself countless times. It breaks my heart that we are so often so very cruel with ourselves. I know that most of us would never talk to our best friends the way we talk to ourselves. If we did, I'm 100 percent sure that they would stop being our friends.

We tell ourselves that we're flawed, we're broken, we're not good enough, we don't have what it takes. We see others achieving their goals and living good lives. We compare ourselves negatively, and think, "I don't know enough, I'm not good enough, I don't have what it takes ..." We do this for years, perhaps unaware that we have chosen these stories. Living on autopilot, we let these stories run our lives.

Rather than living in this negative feedback loop, you have to become your own best friend. No one can pursue meaningful goals when they believe they're inadequate. So you have to learn to like yourself, love yourself, and believe in yourself. And the truth is that you are good enough—you're more than good enough! You are so enough that it's unbelievable how enough you are!

I'm here to tell you that we all have amazing gifts and talents to share with the planet; there are no exceptions. We just need to work on our confidence to be able to step up and be who we came here to be. If you have any doubts about yourself, test them. Set small goals and commit to them. That way, you can start collecting evidence that proves you really *can* achieve whatever you want! Start building that trust in yourself, and you'll start liking and believing in yourself more and more.

HOW TO STRENGTHEN YOUR CONFIDENCE MUSCLES

The first step to changing anything in life is awareness. So, become aware: thoughts are powerful. It's really about paying attention to what our thoughts are, the language that we use moment by moment, and our feelings.

We need to start keeping track of our daily thoughts and experiences. Once we are mindful, we have the power to shift our consciousness and to turn off autopilot.

At first, being mindful doesn't require making any huge shifts. If you catch yourself in negative self-talk, don't beat yourself up! Rather, get excited and tell yourself, "I'm glad I'm becoming aware, I don't have to be on autopilot," or, "I'm getting better because I'm catching it as it happens." Once you're more aware, you may be able to say, "I choose not to go on that negative downward spiral."

Everything is energy. I'm sure you've heard this before, but we all need reminders sometimes. We attract what we radiate, so when we're not feeling our best or we're aware of funky energy, we can consciously and intentionally raise our vibrations. There are specific actions that will uplift our energy; here are some examples.

ACTIONS TO UPLIFT YOUR ENERGY

- Play some music and dance! Move your body. This raises your vibration and makes you more present. (Singing helps, too!)

- Contact a positive friend. This can work wonders.

- Go outside for a walk. Look around and appreciate your surroundings. Connect with nature and the beauty you encounter.

- Sit down and meditate. Create a cozy ambiance by lighting incense or diffusing essential oils.

- Think about all the things you're grateful for—list all your current blessings, even the tiny ones.

- Do a random act of kindness for a stranger.

- Laugh! Watch a funny movie or look for funny videos on YouTube.

- Make a list of your successes and remind yourself of all of your achievements.

In order to shift your negative self-story, you also have to become mindful of the things you *do* love about yourself. Doing so, you allow yourself to feel proud. On the next page, we will explore an exercise designed to help you connect to the things you love and value about yourself.

With an open heart and mind, get out a pen, and give yourself a score from 1 to 5 for each of these virtues, 1 being the lowest and 5 being the highest. Be honest!

Kind	Smart
Generous	Trusting
Disciplined	Loving
Thoughtful	Courageous
Friendly	Loyal
Determined	Optimistic
Considerate	Open-minded
Honest	Imaginative
Ethical	Sensible
Creative	Appreciative

If you scored a 3 or below for any of these, take a moment and ask yourself if you were valuing yourself enough. Where might you be undervaluing yourself? I know deep in my heart that if you're reading this book, you have all of these virtues and more!

Now, I want you to write an "I AM" statement for the three virtues that scored the highest. I want you to take your power back and own them! You can make post-it notes and have them visible as reminders, or you can take a picture of them and have them as wallpaper on your phone, so you will see them often.

"I AM" Statements

I AM _____

I AM _____

I AM _____

I'm sure that at this point, you can see how much we like ourselves directly determines how much other people like us, too. We attract what we radiate. When we love and believe in ourselves, it will transform our lives. As your self-image goes up, it creates a ripple effect in other areas of your life as well.

At the end of the day, the more confidence we have, the greater our ability to live the lives we want. Our hearts' desires are for something beyond where we presently are in our lives. Some examples of this could include: having a successful business, starting your own business, taking that promotion, moving to another state or country, changing jobs, starting a relationship, ending a relationship, etc.

Here's the key: we will require higher levels of confidence to achieve our heart's desires, because our heart will never truly desire something that we're not yet capable of doing. Just know that whatever your heart desires, you can be it, do it, have it.

MORE TIPS TO SKYROCKET YOUR CONFIDENCE

1. *Make the Decision.* Confidence is a part of the Divine package that you already are. You have to decide: are you going to choose the reality of confidence, or the non-reality of doubt, fear, hesitation, inadequacy, and unworthiness?

2. *Learn a new way of communicating with yourself.* Pay attention to what you're saying to yourself, because you're really listening. In fact, what you hear creates your reality. Replace the negative thoughts and see your beautiful unique essence. Start to see who you really are more and more.

65

3. *Start complimenting yourself.* Compliment yourself every time you accomplish something, and every time you do something right. Celebrate it! Start a "Celebrating Me" journal where you can collect evidence of your achievements, no matter how small they are. That way, you can always reach for your journal on off days.

4. *Take loving actions on your own behalf.* Ask yourself, "If I really loved myself, I would _____." Fill in the blank, then do whatever you wrote down! Do this exercise frequently, but most of all, take action.

5. *Give yourself permission to be who you came here to be.* See yourself as a magnificent and perfect expression of life. You're a co-creator with the Universe. Remember that whatever you put out will come back. Self-confidence is created when you are aware of your oneness with Spirit, so let it work with and through you.

6. *Respect your sacred commitments to yourself.* Every time you break a promise to yourself, your confidence takes a BIG hit. Your confidence increases every time you keep a promise to yourself. Make sacred commitments and follow through! That includes setting healthy boundaries with others and respecting those boundaries. Boundaries are your personal power.

7. *Don't compare yourself to others.* You're unique and perfect! Comparing yourself to others will steal your natural joy. Compare your present self with your past self, and look to see how far you've come!

QUESTIONS TO PONDER

- How did you feel while writing the "I AM" statements? Why do you think you felt that way?

- What can you do right now, or within the next two hours, to boost your confidence?

CHAPTER *Four*

Removing the Armor from Your Heart

Removing the Armor from Your Heart

*F*orgiveness is healing. Forgiveness is a gift you give to yourself. Based on my own experiences, I believe that we all deserve to forgive ourselves and others for any wrongdoing. We've all experienced unmet expectations and painful experiences, but when we hang on to them, we keep ourselves from soaring and enjoying our precious lives. Instead, we're weighed down by pain and the burden of feeling betrayed—or whatever else we feel based on our self-stories. But it's possible to let go, and I'm here to tell you that there is no better time than now for sacred personal healing.

It takes work to see which of our self-stories are no longer serving us. We also need to get clear on how it would feel to get beyond them; then, we can finally move on. Forgiving myself and others has made all the difference in my life, because it feels so freeing and liberating!

I often see people stumble and get stuck on a loop because they believe that if they forgive themselves or someone else, it will be as if the initial hurt or betrayal never happened. That's simply not true. We don't forgive someone else for their benefit, and we don't try to pretend that nothing happened. Instead, we forgive for *ourselves*. We do it so that we can move beyond that hurt. When we forgive, we affirm, "I'm still whole and complete. I'm still here, and I can choose to use this as an opportunity to open the door to limitless possibilities. I allow myself to grow and prosper in my life by letting this go."

Here's the thing: by forgiving, we're doing ourselves a favor; we're not doing anyone else a favor. The person you forgive will still have their own karmic debt for all of their actions. However, when you forgive, you're becoming free. When we're focused on resentments towards others or even ourselves, we won't be able to listen to our soul's messages. When we let go, we can tune in more deeply.

Forgiveness takes courage because beneath your personal story of pain and suffering, you always have the choice to access your wholeness, and to tap into your innate joy and compassion. You can learn to forgive yourself and others as you practice letting go of what no longer serves you. Eventually, you will liberate your heart from the resentment prison. You will open to a new way of being and living that you might only dream of right now.

In order to move forward in our lives, one of the key things we must do is release the past. We are growing and evolving spiritual beings who are meant to be living in the present moment. However, we often carry the past with us—and if we're not aware of this, the past will weigh us down, and we will feel stuck. Without a regular practice of releasing, we develop a backlog of unprocessed emotions and mental clutter. This clouds our vision, and can make it difficult to see the next steps toward freedom.

We have all been hurt by the words or actions of others at some point in our lives. The hurt and wounds can leave feelings of bitterness, resentment, and anger for years. We can get to the point that we feel like victims because of what others did to us. When we feel like victims, our feelings are not protecting us, but are rather harming us. We find ourselves locked in emotional prisons filled with hurt. How can we live happy, expansive lives from that place?

Until we forgive, we are the ones paying the highest price. Our trapped emotions can become so overwhelming that they affect our current relationships and our ability to authentically and lovingly connect with ourselves and others. Only when we truly forgive will we be free of pain, hurt, and anger. If we hold on to them, we won't be able to enjoy the present—and they will affect our health in many ways.

The words and actions that hurt us will always be there: unfortunately, we cannot change the past. But we can definitely change how we live our present. Forgiveness is a powerful choice to move on, and to strive for a better life.

This bears repeating: forgiving someone does not mean that we approve of what they did. It doesn't justify their wrong, or mean that we will reconcile. We forgive the person, not the action. Ultimately, forgiving is not for the other person: it is about *you*. When you release and let go, you can live a more peaceful and joyful life. You create a new story for yourself by reclaiming your personal power!

As part of the forgiveness process, you also need to forgive yourself. How do you let go of your thoughts and beliefs about what happened? We may have judgments about our own expectations. We may think about what should have or could have been. However, when we forgive, we have to give up the idea that the past should have or could have been different or better. We can't change the past, so we should not let the past hold us prisoner. Instead, we need to see the hidden value of what happened, because there's always a lesson. As we develop that clarity, we free ourselves from the past and begin to look forward.

BABY STEPS

During my first few months in Spain, even though I knew I had made the right choice, I felt powerless, hurt, sad, and angry—all at the same time. I had so many emotions to process that it was hard to clearly express what I felt. As I told you, I moved in with my parents when I arrived. I didn't want them to see how shattered I was; they had their own issues, and were trying to get settled, too.

I never opened up to my parents or told them the rawness of my feelings. I know they were aware on some level, but I don't think they wanted to hear it, either; it would have been too painful for them. New to Spain and isolated, I had to process a lot by myself. That's why I started to go to the gym, take music and vocal classes, and search for wellness centers where I could share how I was feeling and get holistic treatments.

As I began to heal, I saw how full of anger I was. I had anger towards my ex, of course—but also towards myself for having allowed his behavior. I blamed myself for not standing up for myself more often, for not having had the courage to leave sooner, for allowing myself to be abused for so long, for not seeing the dynamics of my own dysfunction, and for not loving myself enough to know, deeply *know*, that I deserved better in so many ways.

As you can see, I had a lot of forgiving to do.

I found that, in order to forgive, I first needed to experience my emotions fully—to connect with the pain rather than avoid it. After a while, I reached a point where I knew that I could not allow that pain and anger to be key players in the story that would drive my life. I didn't want to believe I was a miserable victim; I'd had a miserable life for a long time already. My practice involved forgiving myself for feeling the pain, forgiving myself for judging myself so harshly and really surrendering to the process: then, I could honor my emotions without resistance.

After months of grieving, the turning point came when I asked myself, "What can I do with this pain and anger? What can I do to turn it into something more positive, so I can finally move on?" I wanted to free myself from the poison of resentment, because I knew I deserved better. At that point, I allowed myself to try new things and began to trust myself again by taking little steps. Having forgiven myself more fully, I rebuilt my trust muscle by trusting myself more and more.

My baby steps included allowing myself to explore painting, keeping up with vocal classes, writing a little bit, and really connecting with my creativity. I also kept going to the gym as an outlet. I meditated often, found a place where I could go for Reiki circles, and found a Buddhist temple where I could go to feel a very deep sense of peace and connection with the Divine.

I'm not saying that my anger and pain evaporated into thin air. I sometimes relapsed into them and found myself sitting on the floor crying my eyes out. But that was part of the healing process, too: I had to honor my emotions and where I was at those moments. Forgiveness was a conscious choice that I made. I got to a point where I really understood that by forgiving my ex-husband, I was freeing myself. By forgiving myself, I was releasing the victim story, and I was taking my power back. As I forgave, I began to love myself enough to remove the walls I had built around my heart, and to open space for new and better possibilities in my life.

As I cared for myself and trusted myself more, a different way of seeing the past opened up before me. Little by little, I started to feel gratitude for all the amazing things that I was doing, and for all my experiences. I began to love myself unapologetically, like never before. I was thankful for my healing journey. Slowly but surely, I discovered who I really was. I forgave myself and everyone else … I was free, and awake.

My journey kept taking me in unexpected directions as I became more and more open. Six years later, at the end of 2009, I was working for a Swiss bank in Barcelona when we all got laid off. The economy was very bad in Spain, and I knew other people who hadn't been able to find jobs for months. Since I have dual citizenship (Spanish and American), I decided to apply for jobs in the U.S. again.

After years of personal development and forgiveness work, meditation, Reiki courses, and massage classes, I felt more grounded and ready to come back to the U.S. I applied for a couple of jobs, and to my surprise, I got a phone interview. After a few days, I was invited to fly to Florida for an interview in person—and I did it. The few days that I was back felt so good! I had always felt Florida was my home.

I knew that if they offered me a job, I would say yes in a heartbeat.

I received an offer, and we agreed that I would start in three weeks. I returned to Barcelona to pack and prepare for my return to Florida. That was in February 2010, and I've been back in the States ever since. I don't regret my time in Spain, because it allowed me to heal and mature, but being back home has been an amazing journey of continued growth.

THE FIRST STEP TO FORGIVENESS

The first step to forgiveness is to connect deeply with your own emotions and pain, and be aware of our thoughts and what we tell ourselves. Honor where you are in this moment, and take ownership of everything that comes up. You can write down your thoughts and feelings on a piece of paper so that you can get clear on what they are.

Then, being totally honest with yourself, ask: how have you allowed those thoughts and emotions to dictate the decisions you have made and the relationships that you have engaged in? How have those thoughts and emotions been running your life?

After you've developed clarity, I invite you to ask yourself the same question that I asked myself: "What can I do with this pain and anger? What can I do to turn it into something more positive so I can move on? How can I start freeing myself from the poison of anger and resentment? What new thoughts do I need to start thinking?"

Maybe you wonder how you'll know that you're ready to begin and embrace sacred healing and open up to new possibilities. The process starts when we choose to allow ourselves to trust again. Are you ready to open up to more joy? To let the people that you love get closer?

You know you're ready when you take a look at your life and say, "This is just not okay anymore. I deserve more." It's a big step:

we often get very comfortable living in pain and our old self-stories. We believe that we can keep the world at bay. I know, because I was there myself for a long time.

This is where we learn to forgive ourselves. Instead of continuing along that all-too-familiar path of discomfort, we have to say, "I'm going to give it a try. I am going to trust myself again; I am going to put myself out there and try new things, because that's what it means to be alive." The willingness to change needs to come from deep inside of us. We find it when we begin to believe that having joyful, purposeful lives full of loving and meaningful relationships is our birthright.

Forgiveness is a conscious decision and a state of mind that we can cultivate through daily practice. It helps us to keep our energy clear. When we embrace forgiveness, we also embrace peace, hope, gratitude, joy, and general well-being. As we embrace it, we also embrace who we are—love. When we forgive, we are retaking power and control over our own lives. Forgiveness gives us freedom. Otherwise, we carry that emotional debt with us!

There are plenty of medical studies that show the link between forgiveness and health. Forgiving can lead to lower stress and anxiety levels, less depression, healthier and closer relationships, a healthier heart, lower levels of blood pressure, lower levels of physical pain, better immune system function, and more. By forgiving, we heal from the inside out!

As you can see, forgiveness has more benefits than disadvantages, so even if you don't want to or feel that it's unfair, forgive everyone and everything, forgive yourself, your thoughts, your beliefs, and your judgments about everything. Start with yourself first if you want, and you will start noticing how a whole new world of possibility opens up for you.

FORGIVENESS LETTER

Writing a letter of forgiveness will transform everything in your life! In my own experience—and in my clients'—this exercise has helped release the negative emotions carried around for years like heavy luggage.

This exercise will help you feel lighter and freer! Once you're done writing your Forgiveness Letter, you can burn it, flush it down the toilet, shred it, burn it, or tear it up. This will help you to release all the charged emotions and energy around what happened, and you'll be able to shift your energy and move forward in life with much more freedom.

Use the example below and fill in the blanks for your own Forgiveness Letter. You can write it to family members, friends, teachers, mentors, and even to yourself!

Dear _____

I forgive you for _____
_____

I understand that you probably thought/believed [list what they probably thought/believed at that time]:

- _____
- _____
- _____

I know that back then I felt [list all the emotions you felt]:

- _____
- _____
- _____

When all I wanted was to [list all of the things you wanted at the time]*:*

- _____
- _____
- _____

I declare that from today on, I know that I am worthy so I choose to provide all of those things to myself.

I understand that today is the perfect time for me to take my power back, because I love myself enough to let go of those old memories and emotions. I choose to be free and happier NOW.

I am choosing to start writing a new story for myself.

I know that by forgiving you, I am allowing myself to reclaim my power, and I'm setting myself free like never before.
Yes, I forgive you, and I forgive myself. There is no emotional debt between us whatsoever, and I celebrate my freedom with a grateful heart!

Signed,

_____

QUESTIONS TO PONDER

- Who would I be without the anger, hurt, and resentment I'm carrying?

- How would my life be different if I forgave the person/ people who have hurt me?

CHAPTER *Five*

The Journey to Your Purpose

The Journey to Your Purpose

O ur lives change when we discover what we really want, and that can only happen when we know ourselves at a deeper level. When we truly know who we are and what we stand for, we can create the lives that align with our deepest desires.

To get to know ourselves, we need to discover our values, gifts, and passions. In addition, we have to become more aware of how we operate, how we react to certain situations or people, and how we go about our days. If we want to live awakened lives, we need to turn off autopilot and get into alignment.

In this chapter, I will share with you some tools that were very helpful for me in finding my own truth, and understanding who I really am and what I stand for.

Before this deep investigation of ourselves, it's important to get into alignment. We're both physical and spiritual, and as I've said before, we are all part of a Divine tapestry: we're always connected to Source or the Divine. When we feel love, joy, peace, gratitude, and creativity, we are in alignment with Source, and with our true nature.

We are born with an internal guidance system: our emotions. If we are aware, they let us know at any given moment whether we're moving towards alignment or away from it. The choices we make based on that feedback take us closer or farther away from what we want in life.

Here are a few examples to help you see this more clearly:

- *When we feel negative emotions such as fear, anger, resentment, guilt, worry, and so on, we are taking ourselves away from Source.* This creates feelings of contraction and a sense of separation from Divine connection. As we perceive this separation, we struggle, and feel like the world is against us. Fear and worry can keep us from making important decisions. For me, these feelings made it difficult to leave my ex-husband and move to Spain. Another example: a client of mine was feeling very overwhelmed about having a conversation with her boss. She hoped to work part-time instead of full-time so that she could have more time to do things that felt in alignment with her passions. Once she had the courage to have that brave conversation, she realized that it was easier than she thought. She took what she knew in her heart was the right step for her, and soon had more time to take Reiki classes, work on her art, etc. But during the time that she was too afraid to begin the conversation, she was anxious and struggled with worry and guilt.

- *On the other hand, when we feel positive emotions such as joy, peace, love, hope, positive expectation, appreciation, etc., we feel an expansive energy that allows us to flow with life.* We respond to circumstances from a more grounded place because we're connecting with Source. This is when we're in alignment. Examples of this include the feelings of joy, appreciation, and hope I felt when I came back to Florida for an interview—as you remember, I ended up getting the job and moving back. (You'll read more about that in this chapter.)

Another client was able to have a heart-to-heart conversation with her husband about how important it was for her to dedicate more time to study, music, and painting. She knew that the joy and peace she felt while doing her art and listening to music meant that she was truly connected to what she was passionate about. She had the conversation with her husband, and he supported her all the way.

Alignment, then, is that state of expansion. And the simplest way to get into alignment is to feel good! Refer to the Alignment Guidance System graphic below. This will bring more awareness and help you understand where you are at any given time when it comes to alignment.

In Alignment - One with Divine Tapestry

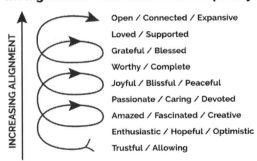

INCREASING ALIGNMENT

Open / Connected / Expansive
Loved / Supported
Grateful / Blessed
Worthy / Complete
Joyful / Blissful / Peaceful
Passionate / Caring / Devoted
Amazed / Fascinated / Creative
Enthusiastic / Hopeful / Optimistic
Trustful / Allowing

Unaligned - Separation from Divine Tapestry

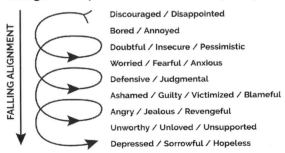

FALLING ALIGNMENT

Discouraged / Disappointed
Bored / Annoyed
Doubtful / Insecure / Pessimistic
Worried / Fearful / Anxious
Defensive / Judgmental
Ashamed / Guilty / Victimized / Blameful
Angry / Jealous / Revengeful
Unworthy / Unloved / Unsupported
Depressed / Sorrowful / Hopeless

I've been studying the Law of Attraction, along with other Universal laws, for over ten years. Something that has worked for me is making time to pause, tune in with myself, and ask myself a few questions. I want to make sure that I'm satisfied with the good that I'm receiving, and with my current experience with life (how life is speaking to me), because I have come to understand that I'm the creator of my own reality.

It's so easy to get off-track sometimes, but at the end of the day, it all comes down to something very simple: *we are nothing but the manifestation of our most prominent thoughts and the images that we hold of ourselves.*

For years, I held a very poor self-image, as well as negative recurrent thoughts that stemmed from that self-image. I never saw myself as pretty enough, smart enough, interesting enough, creative enough, or funny enough. In my head, I was never good enough for anything. That's how I was living my life; therefore, I always felt unfulfilled. I didn't do much to change, so I ended up staying in a dysfunctional marriage for a long time. I was settling for less than I deserved because of my self-image.

I never thought I could have a better life. Sad, right? The worst part is that years went by without me pausing to reflect on who I really was, what could change, or what I could do differently to get different results. I was living life on autopilot: I was unaware and totally out of alignment.

I invite you to take a closer look at the image you're holding of yourself in your mind. That image is the clear manifestation of the thoughts you constantly hold. If you're continuously thinking and talking about how times are hard, how money is scarce, how relationships are tough, how you have no other choice but to stick to your unfulfilling job—that's the kind of seed that you are unceasingly sowing. What kind of harvest are you expecting to get in return?

I challenge you to take the time to check in with yourself and ask yourself this question:

"Am I satisfied with what I'm getting out of life?"

In order to move forward and attract better things, we have to grow and become larger. That means that the images we have of ourselves—who we really are—have to become more expansive than our current images. Basically, we need to do some upgrading.

So, I invite you to ask yourself the following questions to create a shift in your thinking and to open the door to new possibilities:

- *"What do I want in my life?"* In every area of my life, how would I like to feel when I wake up? Grab a piece of paper and write down what you'd like to have in each area. What are you longing for in the areas of:

  - Self-Love
  - Career/Business
  - Health and Fitness
  - Spiritual Fulfilment
  - Family Relationships
  - Friendships and Peer Relationships
  - Romantic Relationships
  - Financial Success
  - Home Environment
  - Societal Contribution
  - Personal Growth

- Now, from a place of curiosity, growth and expansion, ask yourself, *"Who do I need to become in order to attract the experiences that I desire?"* In other words, what would someone have to believe to create the reality that I long for? Notice these words: "From a place of curiosity, growth and expansion." I want you to connect deeply with the possibilities. This is not intended to make you think that you should be there already, or to make you feel that you're not good enough. Don't beat yourself up. The intention of this question is to open up the flow so you can imagine what would be possible for you if you connected with the beliefs you need. Then, you can see your desires become a reality. Finally, you'll achieve them by doing the exercises that I provide in this book, including the self-love and confidence exercises in Chapter Three.

- Ask yourself, *"What opportunities are there around me that will help me achieve what I want?"* Part of the work is staying open to opportunities that come your way without getting attached to the way in which you think they "should" show up. Let the Universe surprise you!

- Ask, *"What's one baby step that I can take today that will get me closer to the things I long for?"* You have to help the process by taking action. Wishing and visualizing alone will not work. You have to do your part and act.

Whatever we have in life today is our own creation, even if we don't like it. But the good news is that we can change it—if we choose to! Always seek for the better, ask yourself questions, and become larger to attract better. When you allow yourself to grow, you let yourself have a better self-image and stay in alignment for longer periods of time. As you begin to use discrimination in your thoughts, you will stop seeing yourself and your circumstances as limited.

Remember, the Universe will give us whatever we ask for—based on what we're ready to receive by being in alignment. Sometimes, we want to have new experiences, but we're not yet in alignment with the state of expansion they would require. When this is the case, we're closing ourselves off to receiving what we say we want; there is no resonance between our stated desires and where we are energetically.

The more we grow, the more our capacity to receive and manifest our desires, and the reality that we long for expands. It doesn't matter how much we pray to get what we want: we won't get it unless we're ready to receive it. We really have to become one with the vibration of what we desire.

We need to start by allowing new possibilities into our minds by holding thoughts that are aligned with a higher and more expansive vibration. We need to get bigger than the life we've experienced so far, and to do that we just need to get off autopilot and start knowing ourselves better. Then, we can manifest the reality we want. When we choose to honor who we were created to be, we practice being in alignment. As we grow, we welcome our new reality.

THE CALL FOR ALIVENESS

In this world, the way society and the media works, many of us try to live up to impossible ideals of happiness. We seek approval and validation outside of ourselves, and compromise the most important thing—being who we really are, being true to ourselves.

In order to be authentic, we need to know who we really are, what we really want, and why we want it. You will not be able to have a better and bigger life if you don't know what you really want. I mean what *you* really want, not what you want based on other people's expectations, or what you "should" like based on your cultural background. Through the exercises in this chapter, you'll start making decisions based on *your own* desires.

Having clarity on what you really want and why you want it will open up the channel to unlimited possibilities and new opportunities. Your "Why" will be the driving force and motivation you need to live the life you want.

Remember, even though we should strive to be authentic, sometimes, we find it's easier to go with what others want us to be or do. It's very challenging to be real in a world that teaches us that, in order to fit in and be liked, we must please everyone at the expense of our own identity and happiness. When we go along with those expectations, we think of ourselves as undeserving of happiness.

However, we always have the ultimate power—the power of choice. Every choice we make, no matter how big or small, matters and has consequences. Deep in our hearts, we know this, and that's what creates the anxiety and fear around making new choices.

The problem is magnified when we don't feel worthy enough to make choices that will serve us. We don't yet believe that we deserve better, and we doubt that we can have what we most desire—be it a better relationship, a better job, etc. With this mindset, we end up settling for less.

Here's the thing: settling for less than we deserve is also a choice. If we conveniently hide behind the thought that we "had no choice," this perfect excuse only leads us to feel powerless. Our inner guidance knows the truth, and going against our core values leads to self-betrayal, which creates great pain. I know this firsthand from my first marriage, and from keeping jobs that felt out of alignment.

The truth is that we're not here to settle for less. We're not here on the planet to shrink and fit in. When we settle and fit in, we're making choices and living life based on other people's expectations. There is no way we will be able to live authentic, joyful lives if we keep "shoulding" ourselves and playing it safe.

In order to be authentic, we have to cultivate the courage to be ourselves, fully—with imperfections and all! We have to believe that we are worthy of love just as we are. We have to be willing to adventure, to listen to our inner wisdom, and to experience our inner power. It's time to *give ourselves permission* to want what we really want, to be vulnerable, and to really believe that being happy is our birthright—because it is!

Being authentic means that you will break up with your old identity to embrace the freedom of who you really are. This chapter is the foundational work that will support you in living an awakened life.

There's something magical that happens when you dare to be your authentic self—besides feeling the freedom that comes with authenticity, you also inspire others to thrive. Everybody benefits when we live life from this place, because being in alignment with our authentic Selves and feeling fulfillment is our true nature. This type of courage has a beautiful ripple effect; those around you will see that they, too, can be authentic.

All this might sound difficult to you now. However, everything in life is course correctable and things can change! It doesn't matter how old we are, or what the situation is—all we need is the awareness of where we are today, the clarity of where we want to be, and the willingness and determination to start making changes in our lives, from today on.

It's time to start making new agreements with yourself and with life! These new agreements will replace the old ones that have kept you playing small and confined you in your comfort zone. I invite you to allow yourself to consciously choose and practice authenticity. Even when it seems hard because fear or feelings of shame and unworthiness surface, you have the choice to live your life intentionally.

Let's discover the areas in which you feel good and satisfied.

THE LIFE WHEEL

By doing this exercise, you can discover if you're living authentically. Your goal is to live in alignment with your soul so that you can create a more joyful and fulfilled life. You will gain clarity on what needs to change and what needs to be released so that you carry only what is essential to living your mission and fulfilling your purpose here on the planet.

Referencing the Life Wheel below, rate your level of satisfaction from 0 to 10, for each one of the areas listed on the Holistic Wheel of Life—0 meaning not at all satisfied and 10 meaning highly satisfied.

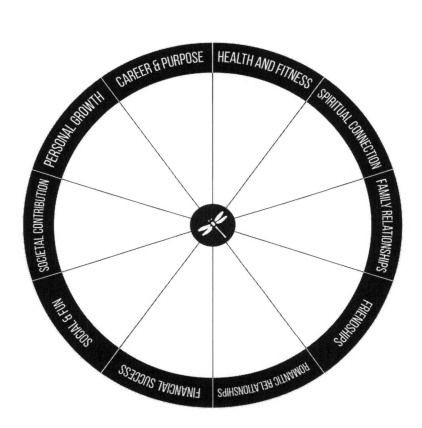

Next, draw a horizontal line across every section. The closer you are to the center of the circle, the lower your satisfaction; the closer you are to the outer line, the more satisfied you are. If that wheel was to turn, how bumpy would your ride be?

UNCOVERING MY CORE VALUES

I had heard about core values before, but I didn't yet know what that term truly meant. Later on, when I started doing even deeper work on myself, I understood that core values speak to what is really important to us.

My first conscious glimpse into my core values came when I decided to return to Florida. My choice felt so right, even though I got some pushback from my family in Spain. They thought I was a little crazy for wanting to come back and make a transatlantic move so quickly and by myself. However, after reflecting, I knew it was the best choice for me.

While on the plane flying back to Barcelona, I made a list of pros and cons for the job and the move. I don't remember every item on the list, but I remember very vividly feeling expansiveness: I knew this choice would help me move forward and learn new things. In addition, the job was about making a difference for people that were having issues with their mortgage loans after the housing bubble burst here in the U.S.

In that very moment on the plane, I realized that advancement, learning, and making a difference were very important to me. Even though my family was a bit reluctant about my choice, I knew it was the right one. On that day, I realized that I was standing up for myself, and making decisions based on what was important to me. My family loved me and had the best intentions, but I knew what I needed. I was no longer paying attention to other people's wishes.

In that moment, it was very clear that this was the way to continue taking responsibility for my own life. My clarity came as a result of all the inner work I had done in Spain. I finally realized that I had been going through life without understanding my own values and without healthy boundaries: this was directly connected to my low self-esteem.

This realization helped me stay more centered and in alignment with my values in the years to follow. I needed to get to the heart of my core values to really start setting healthy boundaries and respecting them. By staying true to my values and boundaries, I was able to stay true to myself. This was the awareness that I needed to recognize the birth of a new story for myself: I broke up with my old identity and made new agreements with myself.

If we want to stay true to our values and boundaries—and ourselves—we have to make a conscious choice to do so every day. Even small choices matter: simple things like choosing self-care and doing things that will bring us joy are meaningful. Choosing to go to a yoga class, get a manicure, or meet friends can help us keep our commitments. By taking care of ourselves and fulfilling our needs, we are filling our own cups.

Living from that place helped me also to get the clarity that I needed when it came to being in a new romantic relationship. In November 2010, I was feeling ready to meet someone new for a long-term relationship, and since I'm not the type of gal who would go to a bar by herself or date guys from the gym, I decided to sign up for a three-month special offer on Match.com. I didn't intend to renew, and I knew that it would okay if I didn't meet anyone that I really liked during those three months.

In the meantime, I had taken the time to get really clear on what I wanted for my next relationship. I had a couple of relationships in Spain, but they didn't work out because I wasn't clear on what I wanted in a partner. So, based on my past relationships, I sat down and made a list of the things that I liked, the things that I would not tolerate, and the things that I would not compromise. I clarified what was important to me, and what qualities I wanted my new partner to have.

94

I was very selective and chose to go out with just a couple of guys. When I realized that they didn't have the qualities I was looking for, I didn't waste my time or energy with them. Then, a week before the membership expired in January of 2011, I received a message. We communicated via e-mail and phone for a few days and decided to meet in person for an appetizer and a drink because he seemed like a good candidate. Now, he's my husband.

One of the first things I told him when we met is that I wanted to get to know him better and become friends first. He took up the challenge. We went out for about six weeks and saw each other a few times a week. I was enjoying the courting process and getting to know him when he finally had the courage to have a conversation about starting to formally date.

He said, "I want you to know that I didn't want to be pushy because you had mentioned that you wanted us to become friends first. But I'm wondering if by taking it so slow you might think that I don't like you, because I do." He showed me that he was really listening and was respectful of what I wanted. That was the beginning of an amazing relationship with him.

We dated for two years and then got married in April of 2013. He's a sensitive, loving, and caring soul with a great sense of humor. He's also a great listener and my cheerleader. Ours is no doubt the best relationship I've had. We respect each other profoundly. In addition, we both love having our own space, but absolutely love spending time together as well. It all became possible when I got clear on what was important to me.

Achieving clarity has made a great impact in other areas of my life as well. In the next chapter, I'll explain how this process helped me honor my unique path despite challenges. For now, keep reading, because we're getting into the heart of what you need as a foundation to get the clarity you long for.

CONNECT WITH YOUR CORE VALUES

Values speak to your true essence: they represent who you are, and what is important to you. Experts who have researched the subject point out that values are so important that some people would rather die for their values than compromise them.

Before I was clear on my values, I felt lost and unfulfilled. I didn't know what I stood for or what was important to me. I was just living life going through the motions, without connecting to who I really am. For me, everything changed once I started knowing myself at a deeper level.

Our core values are like our GPS system or compass: they represent our guiding principles, and they influence how we show up in life. When we truly know ourselves, everything changes. Our self-worth grows, and we live from a more authentic place.

Below is a list of some values that you might find helpful. As you look at the list, notice your reaction to each value. As you read, the values that are most meaningful to you will resonate, and you'll feel a sense of comfort or a deep sense of knowing. This is how you know what is important to you. Place a check mark next to all the values that give you that sense of comfort:

_____	Peace	_____	Honesty
_____	Intelligence	_____	Innovation
_____	Wisdom	_____	Integrity
_____	Spirituality	_____	Self respect
_____	Achievement	_____	Family
_____	Vitality	_____	Loyalty
_____	Security	_____	Learning
_____	Wealth	_____	Order
_____	Pride	_____	Power
_____	Health	_____	Recognition
_____	Community	_____	Accomplishments
_____	Cooperation	_____	Advancement
_____	Creativity	_____	Freedom
_____	Affection	_____	Fulfillment
_____	Making a Difference	_____	Giving Back

_____ Connection   _____ Consistency
_____ Career   _____ Fairness
_____ Beauty   _____ Humor
_____ Growth   _____ Influence
_____ Purpose   _____ Productivity
_____ Pleasure

Now, review the list of values on the previous page. From the ones that you checked, circle the top ten values that truly resonate with you and list them below.

Value #1: _____

Value #2: _____

Value #3: _____

Value #4: _____

Value #5: _____

Value #6: _____

Value #7: _____

Value #8: _____

Value #9: _____

Value #10: _____

If you had to choose one value over all the rest that best describes you, which would it be? Now, you will arrive at five core values in their order of importance to you. Write these in the space below.

Core Value #1: _____

Core Value #2. _____

Core Value #3. _____

Core Value #4. _____

Core Value #5. _____

Post your top five core values somewhere you can see them all the time. Use them as your GPS when you need to make decisions. These will help you stay true to yourself despite any doubts or fears that might show up.

There are many ways this list can help you. Based on the Life Wheel exercise, how can you incorporate your core values in each area of the Life Wheel? How can you start making changes in your life that will align with these core values so that you can live in alignment and add more depth, joy, and meaning to your life?

One more thing: how can you set healthy boundaries with others and yourself so that you can be consistent and live in alignment with your values?

For each one of your five core values, write down the main things that you will not compromise. This will help you be very clear when it comes to honoring your values and communicating what is important to you.

Core Value #1: _____

_____
_____
_____

Core Value #2: _____

_____
_____
_____

Core Value #3: _____

_____
_____
_____

Core Value #4: _____

_____
_____
_____

Core Value #5: _____

_____
_____
_____

GET CLEAR ON WHAT YOU REALLY WANT

I truly believe that we're going through a transformational time on the planet. Spiritually, we're being pushed to align with our life purpose and our souls' callings. It's time to get clear about who we are, what we stand for, and what is important to us, so that we can share our gifts and talents with the world. I've felt this myself, and my clients frequently share that they feel a deep longing inside, an urge to do meaningful work—work that makes them feel alive and that makes a difference.

When we don't pay attention to this longing, we continue to feel stuck. There's a further risk: when we feel that our internal radars are off, we'll look for answers outside of ourselves. As we disconnect from our True Selves, we accumulate layers and layers of fear and guilt. As we've discussed, this leads to living live on autopilot.

In addition, there's an epidemic use of anti-depressants and anti-anxiety medication that are a Band-Aid for the underlying issue of disconnection. I know that some individuals truly need medication, but suppressing who we really are does have consequences. Misalignment will make us feel confusion, despair, and hopelessness. It also creates physical symptoms like anxiety. I've been there myself, and I'll tell you even more in Chapter Six.

Misalignment and confusion can block the changes that our soul might want to make during this time of acceleration on the planet. However, confusion might also be a convenient hiding place. When we're confused, we don't have to take the risks that are necessary for the lives of our dreams.

Confusion comes from a disconnection from our authentic selves. When we haven't been taught to connect deeply with who we really are, we can't access the information we need to get clear about our passions and dreams. Our ego mind will make us look for answers outside of ourselves, imagining that the answer is available in a book or a conversation. In reality, however, the answer is contained inside of us.

I invite you to take some time to pause, connect with yourself, and ask yourself questions. Start paying attention and see how life is speaking to you. See if you feel a longing for something to do, be, or create. What would make you feel vibrantly alive? Pay attention and see if there is a discontent—a constant challenge that makes you feel constricted and closed in.

Our challenges and suffering give us clues. They lead us to what we are here to learn and what we are here to share. We all come to the planet to teach, share, and inspire others—so understanding your own process is key! I invite you to challenge yourself and look at the choices you've made. Are they in alignment with your values? Were you aware of your own values or boundaries?

Paying attention to your longings and discontent provides a great source of information to your conscious mind about what your life purpose is!

Take a moment to explore: if there were no restrictions at all (money, time, age, etc.), what would you do? Remember, always explore putting your focus on your internal world and what's really important to you. Listen to your inner wisdom.

Give yourself at least 15-20 minutes in silence, with no interruptions. You can light a candle, take out incense, or diffuse essential oils. Make the room cozy. Alternately, you could go out and walk in nature. Ask yourself, "If I had a magic wand, what would I do?" Listen to your inner wisdom—your soul. Give yourself permission to know what you already know, and to open up to possibilities. I suggest you use this mantra, which helped me get clear: *"I give myself permission to receive and open up to the wisdom of my soul."*

Pay attention to ideas and images that come to mind. Don't judge or analyze; just be open-minded and allow the flow of ideas.

If your mind thinks about conditions, limitations, or circumstances, simply let your ego-mind say what it needs to, and then bring your attention back to your ideas, mental pictures, etc. Remember, you don't have to think of the "how": we need to get clear on "what" first. Everything else will flow once you get that clarity.

What are your thoughts? Write down your ideas and your mental pictures. Writing down your ideas will enable both parts of your brain to be fully present. By writing it down, you have activated the brain to work on the idea at a conscious and subconscious level.

What I Want:

_____

_____

_____

_____

_____

_____

If this first part was not easy for you, I would suggest that you start by identifying what you *don't* want. Sometimes it's easier to start connecting with the contrast and start getting clear from that place. Feel free to make an exhaustive list in the first column. Be spontaneous: write as much as you want, and use extra paper if needed. Once you have filled in the first column, go through every statement you wrote and flip it to a positive declaration of what you *do* want:

What I DON'T want	What I DO want
Example:	Example:
"I don't want to work for someone else"	*"I want to have the freedom of doing what I love"*

Another technique is to reconnect with the things that give us excitement. Do you remember how creative and passionate we were about the things that excited us when we were kids? Sadly, as we grow older, our ego mind starts repressing our passions. We tend to ignore and neglect the messages from our soul. Instead, we pay attention to external messages like "Be realistic," "That's a stupid idea" "That would never work," "You should do this instead," etc. We let those messages dictate our decisions in life.

In order to reconnect with your life purpose, you have to be able to connect with your passion. This is such an important step in the process! Your passion will give you a direct link to your life purpose. When we stop listening to external messages, we can tune in more deeply and discover our passions.

So start thinking: what are you passionate about? Do you like dancing, exercising, cooking, photography, painting, writing, singing, playing an instrument? Once you've started, get specific. For example, if you come up with a passion like "being in contact with nature," dig deep: what about nature? Is it being in contact with animals, flowers, or trees—or appreciating sunrises and sunsets?

List your passions in the space provided on the next page.

My Passions:

_____

_____

_____

_____

_____

_____

Another way to connect with your passion is by paying attention to how you feel passion in your body. Sometimes we forget that our bodies give us boundless feedback about our feelings and emotions.

A great exercise that can be very helpful is to journal about how you feel passion in your body. What are the particular sensations you feel? Where do you feel them in your body? How do you know when you are passionate about something? When you connect with the feeling of passion in your body, you'll be able to get more clues.

Begin to include the things you are passionate about in your daily routine. The more you respect and honor your passions, the more you will be in alignment and experience joy and creativity. You will open the door to more ideas to come, and let your soul express itself. Eventually, it will reveal your life purpose with full clarity.

CONNECT WITH YOUR GIFTS

We all come to Earth with unique gifts and talents. When you pay attention and see the people around you—creatives, artists, etc.— you notice how amazing, magical, and beautifully unique we all are, and how much we shine when we give ourselves permission to honor and express our gifts.

However, we are often unaware of our gifts. Some of us know that we have talents, but don't know how to use them. In fact, we're not raised in a culture where we are asked, "How can you use your gifts to make the world a better place?" We're usually asked, "What will you do for a living?" When we're young, this confuses our souls, because our souls don't think in those terms.

Within our culture of fitting in, some people are not conscious that they're blocking themselves from shining the way they're meant to be shining. Every human being possesses great treasures waiting to be discovered and claimed. Some people are fortunate enough to naturally use these gifts beginning in childhood, but the majority need to develop awareness of the limitless possibilities we have to create whatever we want in life using our gifts.

We tend not to realize that the things that come easily and naturally to us are our gifts. You might not have an extraordinary voice or an incredible ability to paint, but we all have our own unique gifts. Perhaps you're great at taking photos, or you have a great eye for decorating, or you get compliments about your cooking, etc. All of these are gifts. However, we sometimes think that if something is easy, it is not unique enough to be a gift or a talent, and we may devalue it.

Think of the things that come easily as little seeds that have been planted in your heart. You've been gifted with those talents, and they are clues to the bigger picture. Give yourself permission to nurture them. Take the time to develop them and become better—but please, don't expect perfection. Just allow yourself to explore and experiment with different ways of expressing your gifts.

We must also be sure not to fall into comparison. Measuring ourselves against others will not only steal our natural joy, but will also prevent us from connecting with our own gifts. Everyone is different, so we need to appreciate our uniqueness just as we can appreciate someone else's talents. When we try to be like someone else, we're not honoring who we were created to be.

There is another type of gift: gifts that are innate, but that aren't being fully expressed. The way we know we have these is that we sense a huge potential inside of us that feels untapped. We know that we are capable of so much more than what we are doing now. I certainly felt this way a few years ago, when I was working for corporations and didn't know myself at a deeper level. I knew that I had so much potential. I longed for a bigger and fuller life, but I was not sure of what my gifts were.

How do you identify your gifts?

1. Think of comments that people have made to you over the years. For example: "You are so _____."

2. Try to remember what came naturally to you and what you loved doing when you were a kid.

3. What have other people been able to rely on you for?

4. Interview those that are the closest to you—the people who love you unconditionally—and ask them what they feel are your top three strengths and talents. They will clearly see what might not be so obvious to you.

The following quote made me cry when I read it for the first time. It made a real difference for me, and that's why I'm sharing it with you. In *You 2*, Price Pritchett writes:

You have many gifts that you've never opened. These are gifts of talent, ability, and 'reach' that are yours for the taking. The people we call gifted are different from the crowd in one very special way. They accepted their gifts. They 'let it happen.' The high achievers, the persons you admire, are those individuals who opened their gifts. These winners have more gifts because they claimed them, took them out of the wrapping, and used them.

I invite you to begin to get a sense of what your gifts are, and to experiment with them. It's your time to break out of the cocoon like a butterfly so that you can open your wings and fly! The world needs your gifts now more than ever! Here's one more tip: *your purpose in life can be ignored, but it can't be denied.* It's always there and only you have the power to choose to live it!

Your life purpose is the intersection of your passions and your gifts. Write down what you feel to be your life purpose after all the exploring we've done so far:

_____

_____

_____

_____

_____

_____

It's very important that you don't feel pressured or rushed to give up your job to begin exploring your passions and gifts, unless you have some type of financial security. Leaving everything behind without clarity or a plan will create a lot of stress, and you will not be able to explore if you're living in fear, worry, and scarcity. You can't stay open to possibility when you're focused on merely surviving.

Think about it: keeping that job will provide the funding you need to do more of the things you love. That will pave the way for you to get what you need and create a foundation before you make any bigger decisions and take bigger steps. Clarity will begin to unfold as you start taking those small steps with faith and conviction that you're being divinely guided and supported.

I want to make clear that following your passions and living your purpose can be done every single day by doing things that make you feel more alive and that fill your heart with joy—be it volunteering, creating things, helping others in need, etc. Living your purpose doesn't necessarily mean that you need to make money and support yourself financially through your passion. That may seem ideal, but living life ON purpose can be lived and breathed every day, even if we start by taking baby steps.

Remember: whatever you desire, you can create! You wouldn't be given the seed of a dream in your heart if you were not able to fulfill it. Start thinking of all the ways that your gifts and talents can help bring a better consciousness to the world and create a positive impact.

I love this quote from Joan of Arc: "I'm not afraid, I was born to do this."

At the end of the day, we are all being used as vessels of love by the Divine. We're here to be vehicles of service so that the power of the Divine can work through us. So, I invite you to step aside and open yourself up to be used by the Divine. When you have the courage to start living in alignment with who you were created to be, you will begin to experience freedom, fulfillment, and joy.

Also, it's very important to remember that, as you grow and evolve, your sense of purpose will change. Know that this is normal. Stay open to the process, trust it and flow with it, because life is all about growth and change. Enjoying the journey as it evolves will bring you to the next level of fulfillment so you can continue sharing your gifts and talents with the world.

QUESTIONS TO PONDER

- How do you feel about the work you've done to identify your purpose? Do you feel excited? Scared? A bit of both?

- Have you already been doing or exploring some part of what you were born to do? Where has your purpose already shown up in your life?

- Now that you know (or are getting to know) your purpose, how will your life change going forward?

CHAPTER *Six*

Your Miracle Path

Your Miracle Path

*I*n the past, I haven't always believed in myself or trusted myself. I haven't always felt good enough. I've had to learn how to honor who I really am, as well as my passions and gifts, in order to be authentic. However, I think this is truly common for every human being at some point in life.

I got to the point where the pain of ignoring the messages from my soul was becoming intense and unbearable. One day, while crying, I asked myself the following questions:

- "If I don't trust myself, how can I be sure that I'm willing to really embrace life in all its depth?"

- "If I don't trust myself, am I not trusting the Divine, the Universal tapestry that I'm part of?"

- "If I don't trust myself, am I not honoring my own unique path?"

- "If I don't trust myself, am I not trusting life and the Divine process of the Universe/God?"

- "If the Universe/God knows exactly what I need and when I need it, wouldn't that help me to trust the process and recognize my true nature as a spiritual being?"

113

When I asked these questions, I discovered that many of these feelings have a common root. When we distrust ourselves, lack belief in Divine support, or feel separate from the wholeness of the Divine tapestry, it's often because of shame. We feel that we're not good enough.

As Brené Brown writes in her book, *The Gifts of Imperfection: Let Go of Who You Think You're Supposed to Be and Embrace Who You Are*, "Shame brings up two main stories: never being good enough, or 'who do think you are.'" These stories come from our own old stories, old conditioning, and the agreements we have made in the past.

With that awareness, we can begin to use discomfort as a sign that we're off track. We can do, be, and have whatever we want; we just need confidence in ourselves. When we are in-flow with life, we see that we are always divinely supported.

However, sometimes, when things don't work out the way we want them to, we fall into a downward spiral. We start feeling like victims. When we feel unsupported and undeserving, old wounds can get reopened. Nonetheless, even if we don't see it in the moment, we are *always* supported and guided. To reconnect with this truth, we only have to pause, stop resisting life, and try to trust the process. We have to surrender.

Everything always works for our highest good. Usually, a detour or a stepping stone was exactly what we needed to move forward and heal or learn something that would open up the channel for more goodness in our life. It can be hard to see this while we're in the middle of it.

However, we wouldn't be given the seed of a dream in our hearts unless we have the capacity to fulfill it. Even though we might experience delays, discouragement, and frustration, I am convinced that this is a necessary part of the process. They prepare us for the growth and expansion that's coming! But sometimes we're too busy resisting, stuck thinking on how we think things "should" work out, and we miss the lessons and the blessings that are coming.

LEAVING MY OLD LIFE BEHIND

Getting clarity on my core values was essential in my journey. When I discovered what was important to me, my passions and my gifts opened the door to a new world in front of me. I felt that I was living life on my own terms for the first time—but it took some time, and it was a process.

Back in 2013, I was very happy in my relationship, and I got married in April of that year. But professionally, I was very unhappy. The process of getting clarity on what I wanted to do in my career was painful and confusing. Furthermore, I felt I didn't have too many options: I was in my mid-forties already. Was it too late for a career change? I felt trapped.

I worked for a big bank in Fort Lauderdale, and I felt drained all the time. I was getting sick easily, and I was experiencing anxiety. I sometimes even had panic attacks at work. This made me miserable because I knew that I had a great relationship and a great job. I lived in a beautiful place, too—but I still felt like I was missing something.

I longed for meaning and fulfillment, because deep inside I knew there was more to life than working to collect a paycheck. Seeing the people around me live on autopilot was also very troubling to me. It was an uncomfortable process; I was grateful for all I had, but at the same time, I felt guilty and ashamed for wanting more.

The longing had been getting stronger and louder for a few years. It was an urge that I could not ignore anymore; I felt that I had the responsibility to make my existence on this planet valuable. I yearned to make a difference, and to inspire others to do the same.

In Chapter One, I shared with you that two of my friends unexpectedly passed away from cancer just two months apart in 2013. This was devastating, as well as a huge catalyst for me to take action and start honoring my own path. I realized that I didn't want to leave this world without doing my part and making a difference.

I started questioning my own mortality, and began to truly

understand that the only certainty in life is that we will die. It doesn't matter if we avoid the subject or think that it will happen later in life. We need to stop lying to ourselves and face the fact that we never know when our time here expires. I decided that I needed to embrace that reality, and I started seeing this temporary time here on the planet as a gift that needs to be lived more boldly.

This doesn't mean that I took a leap of faith and quit my job to start figuring out what I wanted to do right away. I just took the time to work on myself. I invested in coaching to get support and the clarity that I needed and was longing for. It took me a few months to get clear on what felt right as my next step.

As I was going through this process with my coach, I also realized that I am a Highly Sensitive Person (HSP), and that made so much sense! This term was coined by Dr. Elaine Aaron, a clinical psychologist, in the 1990s. Being Highly Sensitive is an innate trait that is found in about 20 percent of the population.

Some of the things that indicate that I'm an HSP are that I was shy—and called shy and quiet even by my family members—when I was a kid; that I can't tolerate violent shows or movies; that I always enjoy delicate or fine scents, sounds, and works of art, to the point of getting emotional; and that I always felt that I had a rich and complex inner life as compared to my peers. There are many other characteristics that may indicate you are an HSP.

HSPs are more aware than others of subtleties, mainly because our brains process information and reflect on it more deeply.* That's why we also get more easily overwhelmed: when things are too intense, complex, or chaotic, we become overstimulated.

I knew I was not able to handle everything on my own. There were too many emotions in the mix and too many fears. However, being open to the self-discovery process made a big difference for

*If you want to learn more about Highly Sensitive People (and whether you might be one). visit www.HSPerson.com to take the self-test.

me. I knew things needed to change and I was not sure how, so I looked for support.

When I did my research, I understood that it was okay to receive help. I saw testimonials from people who had gotten support. They shared how they were feeling before, and how getting support helped them to move forward and get the clarity they needed. That gave me the confidence to know that I was not alone, and that there was a light at the end of the tunnel.

As I was allowing myself to be supported and guided, I started understanding more about what was important and what really mattered to me. I reconfirmed that what I felt called to do was to make a difference and help others. Then, not too long into the process, it hit me! What I was meant to do was to support other Highly Sensitive and spiritual women find fulfillment in life.

I understood that my own struggle had a purpose! As I shared with you in the exercises from Chapter Five, I understood that our struggles, challenges, and longings play a very important role in what we are meant to be doing. They can lead us to what we are here to learn and what we are here to teach or share with the world.

And so, baby step by baby step, I started honoring my unique path ... and here you are, reading this book because I had the courage to pay attention and listen to my discomfort. I was brave enough to say, "Enough is enough! I need help and I need to do something about this, because there's no way that I can continue living life on autopilot. There's no way I can continue living the Big Lie. I won't be just one more brick in the wall!"

YOUR PATH OF PURPOSE

As you know, honoring our unique path starts when we get super clear on what we want and what is non-negotiable in our personal lives and careers. Then, we get clear on what is negotiable, and where we are willing to compromise. When we are clear with ourselves, it makes it easier to be consistent, and we are able to have brave conversations with other people as well. The key is to be decisive about our boundaries and to stop making exceptions so that we can keep our promises and honor ourselves.

As we get clear, we may feel we need more support to move in the right direction. In my three years of work with clients and my lifetime of conversations and experience, the most common message I've heard is, "I'm ready for a change, but I'm not sure what my passions are, where to start, or what direction is the best one to go in."

I've found that some people have an idea of what they love and what their passions are, but they lack the support they need to discover where to start and how to go about making the changes they need to make. Without guidance, they tend to stay where they are for years. This saddens me, because I was there myself for years. I relate to the feelings of pain, overwhelm, confusion, fear and frustration—and I am here to tell you that you don't have to wait to start making changes.

In my case, anxiety and the death of my friends were the catalysts that jolted me out of my stuck place, but everybody experiences the need for change in a different way. Some clients have experienced anxiety, and others have had a numbness towards life that has become unbearable. Either of these feelings may affect other areas of our lives, like our relationships. Making changes to move past these feelings is part of the commitment to your own growth and expansion.

Because this book is here to support you in living life *on purpose* and reconnecting with what makes you feel more alive, I'll share with you some information and tips on how to get unstuck from the rot of an unfulfilling job. Please bear in mind that this could be applied to other areas of your life too.

A lot of people spend years developing careers that appear to be fulfilling on the outside. However, very often, at some point—usually in midlife—we long for more. Many people realize that their careers come up short. They recognize that their professional life is missing a few vital elements, and they feel a sense of lack, so the work they do is unfulfilling, purposeless, inauthentic, and out of alignment with who they really are. This was my case, and I've seen this with clients as well.

Some of the common reasons why people feel dissatisfied with their careers, and which trigger that longing for more meaning and making a difference, are:

- They feel their jobs provide very little meaning or purpose

- They feel they don't make a difference or contribution in a big way

- They feel constantly unappreciated and/or mistreated

- They don't think they make enough money to support themselves and their families

- They don't feel they are fairly compensated for the time and the level of responsibility they take on at work

The general sentiment among these people is that it's too hard to keep going to work every day and feel motivated. I know this was something I felt. In many cases, work feels like a drag, so some people tend to change jobs frequently because they are looking for that feeling of satisfaction.

They don't know what they want; all they know is that they don't want to continue feeling this way. But here's the thing—until we figure out what we are passionate about and what makes us feel alive, we will continue to struggle. I know this too well; it was part of my own journey!

If you don't do something about this feeling of dissatisfaction, you will continue to feel stuck, and you'll hold yourself back from your dreams. This will make you feel that your internal radar is off, and you'll look for answers outside of yourself, because you have become disconnected from your center—your true Self. As years go by, there are layers and layers of fear and guilt that have accumulated, so eventually, some of us bury our dreams and purpose, and go through life without living from an authentic place.

Fear holds us back and, sadly, some people keep surrendering to the status quo, because keeping that job is "what we're supposed to do." However, staying confined to that office or cubicle and submitting to the clock-in-clock-out often leads us to feel overwhelmed and trapped. It's like enduring a slow death.

Some people know, deep in their hearts, that there's something else to life because that feeling of longing for something more meaningful gets stronger and stronger. This is a signal for growth and expansion; we just need to listen carefully to what our souls are telling us and start taking action to get the clarity we need.

Think about it from a holistic point of view: we spend so many hours of our lives doing something that we don't love that at some point, that dissatisfaction gets into us and starts creating a ripple that affects other areas of our lives (our health, relationships, etc.). Then, our level of joy and fulfillment becomes very low.

When we're not energetically aligned to who we came here to be, we continue to struggle. When we give ourselves the permission to break away from the herd, to connect with our inner wisdom, and to allow ourselves to want what we really want, we lead ourselves to the highest levels of joy—faster than anything. The truth is that we're either living *on purpose*, or we're hiding behind our fears.

So, I invite you to pay attention to the dissatisfaction, the anxiety, the fear, and the confusion. Allow yourself to be open and welcome those as signals from your soul—your True Self—letting you know that you're ready for growth, expansion, and the bigger life that you deserve. As I said before, I'm not suggesting that you quit your job today … all you need to do is start taking baby steps to get the clarity you need, so that you can start living *on purpose*.

The only things that prevent us from achieving our dreams and getting what we really want in life are the excuses we make for ourselves. These stories, based on fear, will block any chance that we have to live authentic lives, aligned to our life purpose.

Awareness is key, so be mindful of what you're telling yourself. If needed, revisit the "Confidence" section in Chapter Three. The key here is to believe in yourself and s-t-r-e-t-c-h beyond your fears, keeping in mind that the only way to get different results is by trying new things and taking new risks. In addition, remember that we're always divinely loved and supported.

I want you to imagine for a moment and give yourself permission to think of all the wonderful benefits of working towards your dreams and living your life *on purpose*. Here are some that are worth the effort:

- You would be living from an authentic place, owning your own story, and living life on your own terms.

- You would be providing an amazing example to your kids by encouraging them and those around you, really showing them that it's possible to live life while being true to yourself.

- Your relationships will improve in a magical way.

- Your days will be filled with more energy, meaning, excitement, and enthusiasm.

- Nothing will bring you more joy and freedom in life than living aligned to your True Self and your life purpose.

Ultimately, living the life you came here to live, and being who you came here to be—giving your greatness to the world—will create a beautiful ripple effect that is *so* needed nowadays!

121

THE KEYS TO FULFILLMENT

We all want more in life. We want to achieve our deepest desires, express who we really are, live with purpose, and realize our highest abilities. But how do we achieve self-fulfillment?

Fulfillment comes when we know who we really are. This doesn't mean identifying ourselves with external roles like being a mom, a lawyer, a CEO, a wife, etc. We come to know ourselves when we go beyond the ego, and see ourselves as perfect, whole, and complete spiritual beings whose natural states are love, joy, and freedom.

Fulfillment arrives when we make the choice to go on an inner journey and become aware of what we really want and what we stand for. This requires us to listen to the voice of our True Self—the soul, not the ego. All of the conditions that allow the ego to feel fulfilled are external, and we don't have control over many of those factors. When we focus on ego-fulfillment, we feel frustration, self-judgment, and fear. We compare ourselves to others, and as a result, we fall into the sense of separation that I discuss throughout the book. This sense creates struggle and suffering for all of us.

We will also feel fulfilled when we decide to dive in, explore, and become clear on what direction to go in. When we do this, we connect to the Divine and begin to come from a place of enthusiasm, expansion, inspiration, joy, and deep knowing. When we have this kind of clarity, our awareness is always open, and we know what it is that we want to nurture. We also discover what is meant to be released because it's no longer serving us and is not allowing us to grow and expand.

So, how do we tune into our soul's desires and purpose and tune out from our ego? We have to connect to our authentic self through meditation and quiet time on a daily basis—not just to quiet our thoughts, but also to detach from them. Then, we learn to trust that we can be safe if we let go. This way, we can listen to our inner wisdom and awaken ourselves to what really matters: connecting with Spirit and our spiritual selves, and being vessels of Divine love. With this awareness, we can serve from this place, instead of feeling discouraged by external circumstances or events.

When we make the inward journey and understand fulfillment from this point of view, we clearly see the holistic connection between our True Self and the path of fullness that leads to a happy, successful, purposeful, and abundant life.

As you become more aware on your journey, pay attention to signs, possibilities, and opportunities. A lot of synchronicities happen when our attention and intention are set in motion. I invite you to ask yourself:

"How will I let my life be enriched by all the possibilities that always surround me?"

When we honor ourselves, we are being brave. We may still have some inner stories running in the background that tell us we are broken or unworthy of achieving our deepest desires. However, when we decide to show up this way in life *despite* our inner stories, we get a deep sense that there is complete wholeness behind that supposed brokenness. It was such a relief when I realized this!

At the end of the day, the risk of not showing up in life is great. When we stay in a place of fear, we believe that some parts of us are still unworthy of being shared. In truth, if we don't share the parts of us that have been crushed and feel inadequate, we'll miss out on the opportunity to live life authentically and to the fullest. When we show up in a genuine way, we feel fulfilled, and we are able to make a difference and inspire others.

After losing my two friends to cancer, I decided that I don't want to look back on my life with regrets one day. Here's the thing: there is an incredible loss when we don't follow our purpose and allow ourselves to be who we were created to be. There is our own loss of joy when we don't follow our passions, or when we don't honor and share our gifts—and there is also the loss of the people who miss out on what we came here to share.

QUESTIONS TO PONDER

- What is it costing you not to have clarity on your own truth and the dreams you want to achieve? What are you missing out on?

- What does it mean to you to feel fulfilled? What is the source of fulfillment in your life? What feelings do you associate with fulfillment?

- How congruent is your life? Is it aligned with your vision of fulfillment? Or is it way off-base?

These questions really help us identify the gap—and what it will take to feel fulfilled.

YOUR "WHY"

When we get some clarity on what we want to do, we tend to want to know *how* we will make it happen. But, the first thing we need to ask ourselves is *"Why* do I want it?" Your "why" will be connected to your core values, passions, and gifts.

When we connect with our "why," which is our driving force and motivation for what we really want, something magical happens. Getting clear on our "why" puts us in direct connection with the vibration of our bigger and fuller life.

We can use our "why" as our compass to make decisions and take inspired and aligned actions so that we can get closer to living our missions.

As we get more and more aligned to our "why," we will start to see the *how* shows up magically in our lives. We will start witnessing synchronicities and opportunities that will show up out of nowhere. We'll receive ideas, resources, and more.

Write down five reasons "Why" you want what you want. You can do this exercise for each of the areas that we covered in Chapter Five. That way, you'll be super clear on why you want those things in your life.

"Why" #1: _____

_____

_____

"Why" #2: _____

_____

_____

"Why" #3: _____

_____

_____

"Why" #4: _____

_____

_____

"Why" #5: _____

_____

_____

To get even more clarity about why you want to achieve your desires, I invite you to think about the ripple effect. Ask yourself this question: "What would the world look like if I achieved my dreams?"

Write five reasons why the world would be a better place if you achieved your dreams:

Reason #1: _____

_____

Reason #2: _____

_____

Reason #3: _____

_____

Reason #4: _____

_____

Reason #5: _____

_____

If at some point you get stuck on the how, come back to these lists of "Whys." Stay open to possibilities and opportunities; sometimes we get guidance in the subtlest ways. We may overhear a conversation, read an article, see a billboard while driving, or receive advice from someone we know. We just need to be open to seeing these subtle messages and signs that are guiding us every day.

MANAGING YOUR PRECIOUS EMOTIONAL ENERGY

With TV and the radio, we all know that the frequency or station we are on will determine the picture or the music that we'll get. If we tune in to a station that transmits bad news, that's what we will hear. If we tune in to a station that plays classical music, that's what we will hear.

The same happens in our lives: we get results depending on what dial we are tuned to. We attract what we radiate. The more we align our thoughts and emotions with a higher frequency, the more we are open to all possibilities.

We'll never do what we really want to do, or get where we want to get in life, if our minds are tuned to perceive our current conditions or circumstances as limitations. If our minds are tuned to believe in possibility, the results will be different. We tend to think that we will be able to do what we want only when conditions change (i.e., when we retire, when kids leave for college, when we get out of debt, when we get a better job). But the reality is that our perception of those conditions will start to change once our thoughts change and we start taking different actions.

When it comes to moving ourselves to a higher vibration, it all starts with our thoughts. If we want a frequency that is more about feeling in flow, getting ideas and answers, or feeling passion and inspiration, we need to become aware that we're part of something bigger: a higher power, a Universal mind—the Divine tapestry. Have you realized that you wouldn't even be here, alive and breathing, if you weren't part of it?

It's also important to remind ourselves and acknowledge that we are one with the Universe/God/Spirit/Divine. Even when we experience challenges, we are connected to this infinite power. All the answers are already there for us if we are willing to connect within. When we are open to see that there's always a solution for every challenge, and to trust that the support and love from the Divine is always bigger than any problem we might have, we automatically shift ourselves to a higher vibration. We are in flow with life.

Every day, we are exposed to multiple sources of information and external issues that trigger the conditioned part in us. Some examples include encounters with family members, people at work, society, our culture, and the media. We are constantly bombarded with information and demands from our culture to measure up to certain pre-established standards.

That's part of being human and living in this world and era, but it can be very exhausting and draining. It creates an internal struggle and our ego-mind gets louder, often leading us to feel anxious, depressed, and stuck. We may even feel like victims of other people or of our circumstances. That's why we need to keep reminding ourselves that we are one with the Universe. Then, we bring ourselves back into alignment.

ELIMINATE TOLERATIONS TO MAKE ROOM FOR YOUR DREAMS

In order to move forward, have a more balanced life, and live our dreams, one of the key things we must do is release what we are tolerating in our lives. One way to get clear on where we're going in our life, career, or business is to know where we are today.

Getting clear on our present can be difficult because it requires that we are fully honest with ourselves. Therefore, we need to approach this exploration from a place of curiosity, and to be open, gentle, and kind with ourselves so that we don't fall into the trap of self-judgment and comparing ourselves to others.

So, I'm asking you … Where are you today? Because the truth is that the seeds of your future are sown in the present moment.

I know that many people struggle to manage their day-to-day lives. With our busy lifestyles and all those to-do's, there are many days on which there is little or no energy left to create momentum. Even though there may be deep longing in our hearts, it is difficult to take the inspired actions that will lead us closer to living our dreams.

Many people struggle with time management, and the truth is that we can't manage time. We can, however, manage our choices, priorities, and energy.

It's so simple but so true: in order to live your dreams, you need to make room for them in your life. The way to make room is not by creating more hours in the day, but by making different choices and shifting your mindset. This allows you to free up energy that you can use to go after your dreams.

One of the keys to success is taking personal and energetic responsibility, because at the end of the day, the lives that we're living now are the direct results of our own creation.

Here are some tips for shifting the way you manage your energy:

- *Get clear on how you spend your precious energy.* Knowing where your energy is going will help you avoid feeling scattered. When your energy flows in many different directions, you may end up exhausted at the end of the day, or feel that you accomplished little. By developing awareness, you can begin to make new choices.

- *Take an inventory of the parts of your day.* What energizes and refuels you the most? Which part of the day drains your energy? You only have so much energy available each day, so it's important to study how you are currently using it.

- *Pay attention to your thoughts, feelings, and actions.* The thoughts and beliefs that you have now are the predictors of your future. Ask yourself, "What beliefs do I need to let go of to open myself up to experience my vision fully?" Your future is built from what you think and do now.

- *Start to acknowledge what you are tolerating.* Awareness leads to freedom. What are you tolerating even though it distracts you and drains your energy? Some examples could be: things around you that don't reflect who you are anymore (i.e. wardrobe items, decorations at home); friends or family members that you have outgrown; activities that are not aligned with what's important to you, but that you do out of guilt or shame; staying in situations that no longer fit who you are; etc. Create a list of everything you're tolerating, because sometimes, the act of writing it down is a step towards its releasing! Use a holistic approach and consider the following categories: physical environment (home, office, car), personal finances, relationships (hint: review your boundaries), health and well-being, career, and play time. Create this list from a place of curiosity, not from a place of judgment, and pick from one to three items at a time, so you can work on releasing those tolerations. When you're done, come back to your list for more.

- *Celebrate your new level of awareness* and trust that every toleration on your list has a solution to be found! Also, be open and willing to delegate, ask for help, or outsource when needed. Do it for your dreams and for the ripple of good that they will create!

Without a regular practice of releasing what we're tolerating, we may develop backlogs of unprocessed emotions, unhealthy boundaries, and physical and mental clutter that tend to cloud our judgment. This clutter keeps us from growing and will squash our creativity.

Just know that there's a difference between tolerating something and surrendering to or accepting something. There are certain things that you can eliminate from your life, meaning, you have the choice and the power to make different decisions that will bring more growth and that will help you live in alignment with your truth. Unfortunately, however, there are some things in life that we can't control, and that we just have to accept or stop resisting. Even in these situations, we can choose how we are going to respond and use our energy.

Every little thing that you tolerate is draining your precious energy. Once you start releasing some of the things on your list, you'll feel lighter and you'll be able to make different choices on how to use your energy more productively, so you get closer to your vision, have a more balanced life, and create the life of your dreams, *intentionally*.

Just as with the rest of life, it's a matter of choice. We are always creating and re-creating in life, whether by design or by default. One thing is for sure, we don't get to *not* create.

Have you ever thought about how fortunate we are that, as human beings, we have the consciousness to know that we can choose whether we will look at the upside or downside of things? We can't control some circumstances, but we can control how we deal with them. We either react or respond. The key is to choose acceptance, because it's either going to control you or you're going to control it.

We *always* have a choice in everything we do. The results we get in life are based on those choices. We are the gatekeepers of what goes on in our minds, and in our lives. It's up to us who we decide to surround ourselves with, what conversations we engage in, what we watch on TV, what books we read, how we spend our free time, etc. We are the creators of our own lives—we have the power of choice!

Ask yourself: how are you feeding your mind, your body, and your soul? It's your choice to choose positive or negative, healthy or unhealthy, joyful or painful, expansive or constricted. Be mindful of your choices in your daily activities so you can live to your fullest potential and be the person you came here to be. Choose to live a more balanced and authentic life.

Are you choosing growth, joy, freedom, and expansion? Or are you choosing fear, stagnation, unhappiness, and constriction? Are you choosing to live your own truth and the life you came here to live? Or are you choosing to continue living under the "should" stories? Do you want to feel joyful, or comfortable with your discomfort? Again, the choice is yours!

Life is a beautiful adventure; we know when it started, but we have no certainty about when it will be over. Everything that happens in the middle while we are here on Earth is really on us. The power of choice makes it easier for us to remain true to the core of our being and our own truths.

A few years ago, I read a quote from a Buddhist text on death that said: "Life has a definite, inflexible limit, and each moment brings us closer to the finality of this life. We are dying from the moment we are born." I was a little bit unsettled by it, but when I thought about the meaning of it, I realized that it is pure truth.

Knowing this, we *must* participate in the fullness of life. It's our ultimate responsibility to live life on our terms and to create more balance for ourselves. We try so hard to be happy, to create success, and to feel joy. We tend to make it very complicated, and we look for external things to fill in the gaps. However, in reality, it is very simple. Living well, with joy and without regret, is all about the way we choose to perceive and live everyday life.

I hope you choose to live your life in such a way that you become a living example of possibility for others, and that you do it in a special, sacred, and profound way.

QUESTIONS TO PONDER

- Was it easy or challenging for you to access your "Why"?

- "We don't get to *not* create." How does this statement make you feel? What does it bring up for you?

- How can you choose to perceive your life differently today in order to make room for more joy and expansion?

CHAPTER *Seven*

*The Magic of
Living Your Vision*

The Magic of Living Your Vision

When we create captivating visions of what we want in life, we move closer to finding balance and fulfillment. This is one of the best strategies for achieving the lives that we dream of. When we use our vision as a compass to guide us, we can make decisions and take actions that help propel us towards our bigger and fuller lives. When you create a Life Vision Statement, you create a clear path for yourself to follow.

When I felt overwhelmed because I had to make difficult and scary decisions, I discovered how powerful it is to have a clear Life Vision Statement at hand. My statement is related to my core values. With it, the decision-making process becomes much easier: now, I make decisions based on what is in alignment with the life I want and what is important to me.

One of the traits that all successful and fulfilled people share is that they cultivate passion and enthusiasm for life, and they have a clear vision of what they want. In fact, we all need a compelling vision for our lives, and it has to be powerful. With our visions clear in our minds, we will feel driven to do whatever it takes to achieve them.

To create a vision, we have to begin by identifying our core values, knowing what our passions are, being aware, having a sense of what our purpose is, and having clarity on what we want in our lives. In Chapters One through Six, we completed exercises to get clear on what we want. Now, we're almost ready to put these steps into action.

However, there are a few factors that can get in the way and stop people from creating their vision. Some of the most common are the conditionings that we experienced as we grew up. We were not taught to connect with our heart and make decisions based on what's important to us. As a result, we sometimes limit ourselves and make decisions based on what's in front of us, or what we believe is possible based on our current circumstances. What would it take to look beyond those circumstances?

Visualizing is a muscle that was in great shape when we were kids. We once used our imaginations with no limits—but as we grew up, that muscle atrophied. We were conditioned not to use it. Now, we need to start using that muscle again, little by little, until it becomes stronger.

Fear of the unknown can also get in the way of creating an enticing vision. We may fear that we don't have what it takes, think that we're not good enough, or believe that we're unworthy of dreaming big. These fears and beliefs are a way we give ourselves permission to keep playing small and to stay in our comfort zone. This sometimes even leads us to believe that safety is more important than growth. But here's the truth: the unknown is the doorway to infinite possibilities and freedom!

It's also important to remember that our vision doesn't need to be perfect. There's no such thing as a "perfect" vision. We only need to be open to creating a vision that's true for us; we can see this as part of the self-discovery process that helps us clarify what's important. Also keep in mind that your vision can be tweaked and revisited any time you want.

Our Life Vision Statement will be our expanded "Why." As we create it, we'll be able to get clear on what we want, and all that it entails. We'll look past today and any current limitations as we open our minds to the infinite possibilities of the future. This in turn will give us hope for a bigger and fuller life. Our ultimate vision flows from acknowledging that we all have the right to live a more purposeful life on this planet.

YOUR LIFE VISION STATEMENT

So, how do you create your Life Vision Statement? I invite you to follow these seven simple steps and give it a try.

1. *Pick a place that inspires you* and where you won't be interrupted so that you can tune in with yourself, connect with your heart, and let your soul talk to you.

2. *Don't play small.* Make sure your vision is big enough and interesting enough to get you motivated and excited.

3. *Use Self-Reflective questions.* Ask yourself, "What do I want to create in my life?" Based on your core values, what motivates you? What energizes you? What would you like your life to look like? If you had no obstacles or limitations at all, what would you do? What would you do with your time?

4. *Write down what you want as if you were receiving it in the present.* The mind only deals with the present, the now. So, on a piece of paper or in a journal, you can start by stating, *"I am so happy and grateful now that ..."* As you connect with your heart's desires, do some automatic writing of what your vision is.

5. *Charge your vision with emotion.* Make sure you use words that have the power to move you to action. Some examples are: "Fearlessly, I ...", "Enthusiastically, I ...", "I'm courageous enough to ..."; "Confidently, I ..."

139

6. *Add details.* Your vision should have specifics on the results you want to achieve in your life, as well as the feelings you want to experience. In as much vivid detail as possible and in the present tense, create the life you imagine. Don't waste time and energy trying to make it perfect; just let the writing flow freely and in a way that excites you. Don't overanalyze it, because you might let your ego get in the way.

7. *Create a Vision Board.* A Vision Board is a board on which you paste or collage images that you've gotten from various magazines.* When you surround yourself with images of who you want to become, where you want to live, what you want to do, what you want to have, etc., your life starts changing to match those images and you start achieving your goals. This will add more value and power to the Life Vision Statement because you'll be able to see it and connect with it visually.

Once you've completed the steps, you can consciously reaffirm your Vision by reading your writing every day, and rewriting or updating it as often as is possible. In addition, looking at your Vision Board daily will strengthen the image in your mind. Next time you're faced with a tough decision to make, use your Life Vision Statement and your Vision Board as a compass, and you'll know if your decision will be aligned with your vision or not.

A Life Vision Statement is meant to be lived. I invite you to use these easy tools to step into your greatness and, consciously and

---

*I created a free offering to walk you through the process of creating a vision board. Download the free report here: www.InnerProsperityAcademy.com/visionboard

courageously, choose to start creating and moving into a life you love—the life you came here to live! In addition, always keep in mind that our dreams live in the realm of infinite possibilities!

FINDING MY CALLING

As I shared in Chapter Six, after the death of my friends and the internal chaos that I had been facing about my career, I decided to take some time to work on myself. Everything began to transform when I made the time to get quiet and dig deep.

I had taken courses in meditation, Reiki, and massage therapy, so I already knew that my passion was connected to the holistic and spiritual path. I wanted to help people and make a difference. But at first, I wasn't sure what that would look like.

Since I didn't want to go back to school for psychology, I decided to explore Life Coaching. I enrolled in a Life Coach certification program by the end of 2013. When I was done, I felt I needed more training and guidance. I prayed for a mentor, knowing that I had been in a rut for so long that I couldn't get out of it alone.

At the same time, I was fearful about that internal urge to do something more fulfilling, and I was hesitant to voice what my soul was whispering to me. In addition, I felt that I was too old to start something new, especially something that had nothing to do with the career I'd begun preparing for in college. I believed that I didn't know enough, or that I didn't have enough credentials to coach anyone yet.

I decided to share all this with my husband. When I opened up to him about how I was feeling and what I was being called to do, he was very supportive. He told me that if that's what I really wanted to do, I should give it a try; he wanted me to be happy.

A few days after that conversation, my mentor appeared out of the blue. It was like an answer to my prayers. One day, while browsing Facebook, I saw a post in a group I had joined. I clicked on the name, and I found my mentor. I would go on to earn my Holistic Coaching certification through her program. It was exactly what I'd needed to connect all the dots.

Coaching felt right for me, and being part of that certification program helped me get even clearer on my core values, gifts, and vision. I built more confidence, and started putting myself and my message out there. I felt excited and fired up about being able to support other women going through experiences like mine so that they could live from a more authentic place!

In April of 2014, after completing two coaching certifications, I decided to start my business while I was still working full-time. That gave me a new motivation to show up for work every day; I knew that my job was funding my dream, so I was no longer miserable, feeling that I had no other choice but to continue living life on autopilot.

I was excited that my life had a renewed sense of meaning and purpose. I also received a key piece of feedback that told me I was on the right track. I noticed something very important: my panic attacks were gone. Coincidence? Not at all!

I was finally living in alignment with my own truth and taking steps towards my vision. They felt like taking baby steps, but nonetheless, I felt like my soul said, "Okay, Patricia, now we're talking! You listened and you're taking action … I don't need to get loud and make you feel uncomfortable anymore."

This was a huge lesson for me. We underestimate the importance and depth of the messages that our bodies try to communicate to us. We tend to ignore them because we're immersed in our own stories and living like robots. We miss out on the important information our bodies communicate when we don't take the time to pause. However, when we get quiet and breathe, we can be in the present moment, reconnect with our bodies, and receive their messages.

As I have continued to use my Life Vision Statement as a compass, my decisions have been more aligned with my truth. I make choices based on what feels authentic and expansive rather than on what I think I *should* do. I follow my compass as I decide how I spend my time and with whom, what courses or programs I want to invest in, what new offerings I want to share with my audience, and more.

EMBRACING CHALLENGES

Our Life Vision Statement can be very helpful as we navigate through tumultuous times and life's challenges. Challenges are little tests that we need to pass. Many people give up when they face them, and then never give birth to their dreams. This is why it's so key that, when challenged, we remain committed and keep doing our best, because the little things that can seem insignificant can actually make a big difference.

I've discovered that even when things appear to be stagnant, on the inside, we're growing and preparing. I know very well that we can get discouraged by this process. In those difficult times when we're tempted to give up, we should remember the process of pregnancy. A woman has to go through nine months of changes and discomfort to have a baby. It may be uncomfortable, but it's part of the process of bringing a new life to the world. So please, don't run away from the process: do your part and be willing to go through it.

In addition, keep in mind that the pain caused by our challenges can in fact be healing. I'll give you an example: a fever is a natural mechanism that tells us something needs our attention. We can use this metaphor to consider our challenges: when we feel that our soul is in pain, we should thank it for its message. Then, we can heal or release what needs to be healed or released, and can experience more fulfilling experiences in life.

143

One of the most important keys to bringing our dreams to life is being true to ourselves. We have to trust our vision, believe in ourselves, and trust the process. Being true to ourselves is a conscious choice that we can make over and over again; it's a way of living, where we stay in touch with our inner guidance. When we follow our hearts, all our actions will be aligned to our values and visions.

The only way to be true to yourself is to be self-aware of what you *really* want. You need to know what you want and be aware that wanting it is your birthright. Most of all, you must know that you deserve it. Don't settle for situations that don't honor your truth because this will bring more pain in the long run.

I know that it can be challenging to stay true to yourself in some circumstances. You could face situations and people that want you to compromise your values and what feels right to you. It takes courage, confidence, and determination to believe in yourself, remain on-course, and follow your own path—but it is so liberating!

When you feel challenged, or if you need to find inner strength, just slow down and take the time to connect with yourself. Take a few deep breaths, connect with your inner wisdom, and connect with your vision and your "why." Allow your soul to guide you when you are facing other people's judgments, or even your own. Always keep in mind that what works for other people might not be the best thing for you; we all have our own unique path here.

You are unique, and there is no one like you. No one has the same purpose, the same gifts, or the same passions. Only YOU know what will work for you, so honoring your truth and taking action to fulfill your vision is your responsibility, no one else's.

As we covered in Chapter Six, we need to release what we're tolerating, including any habits, situations or relationships that do not serve or empower us anymore. The key here is to unapologetically love yourself. Do not wait for other people to approve your path. Believe in yourself and listen to your inner guidance: your heart knows the way, and you *can* live your life with meaning and freedom.

It's important to remember that we're always committing to something. If we're not experiencing what we really want, there's a part of us—perhaps an unconscious part—that is fearful, or that doesn't want to achieve it. That unconscious part is like the bottom of an iceberg. We really don't have commitment issues; we're always committed to something, whether consciously or unconsciously.

Awareness is key here, so are you committed to consistency or inconsistency? Are you committed to growth and making a difference, or to hiding and playing small because it's safe?

We've made unconscious agreements in our lives that served us at some point, but we can't experience change and different results without becoming more aware of what we've been committing to. When we become aware, we can finally start making different choices. We change when we consciously commit to ending those old agreements and taking inspired actions that are more in alignment with what we really want. Then, we begin to live life *on purpose* and to fulfill our unique visions.

BLESSINGS IN DISGUISE

Write down one thing that has happened in your life that seemed terrible at the time, but ended up being a blessing in disguise or part of a better picture. Then write down the overall goodness that came from that experience.

_____

_____

_____

_____

_____

_____

_____

YOUR "TO BE" LIST

Every morning, instead of creating a "to-do" list, create a "To Be" list. Write down three things that would go on your "To Be" list for today. You can get a beautiful journal so that you feel inspired to continue this practice each day and focus on your dreams. Creating this "To Be" list every morning will move you closer to the manifestation of a life that is more authentic and aligned to what's important to you, so you can live life *on purpose*.

1. _____

2. _____

3. _____

QUESTIONS TO PONDER

- What came up for you while you were creating your Life Vision Statement and Vision Board? What thoughts and feelings did you discover?

- Do you truly believe that it's possible to create your dream life?

- What small step can you take today to make the life on your Vision Board a reality?

CHAPTER *Eight*

Prosperity from the
Inside Out

Prosperity from the Inside Out

When we hear the word "prosperity," we usually think of financial abundance, material possessions, and external factors that contribute to our happiness and success in life.

But what about "inner prosperity"? Have you ever thought about what that might mean?

Without inner prosperity, we may have financial wealth and material comfort and yet still find ourselves searching to continuously gather more and more superficial wealth. When this is the case, our happiness is dependent on expectations, results, and outcomes outside of ourselves.

It is nice to be financially comfortable and to have nice things—who doesn't like that? However, when you experience inner prosperity, you are connected to your True Self: you're living a life that feels authentic to you and in alignment with your core values. More, you're not driven by fear. You experience inner prosperity when you are guided by your inner wisdom, when you're kind to yourself and to others, when you let yourself be curious and creative, and when you're in-flow with life. Your heart can open and be filled with joy, gratitude, internal peace, self-love, and self-trust.

Inner prosperity begins with the good that we give to the world through our gifts. It is one of the main keys to success, and it starts from the inside. Everything we attract on the outside really does stem from how we feel internally. It creates a ripple effect—all from the inside out.

If we don't feel that we are enough, if we don't value and love ourselves, or if we don't believe in ourselves, we will rely on external factors for our happiness. However, happiness based on material achievement and the approval of others is, at the end of the day, meaningless—all it brings is pain.

If you're not doing it already, make a conscious decision and start cultivating inner prosperity. Just think of the gifts that you have been given. Life itself is a gift! There's always something to be grateful for every day.

Remember, we get to choose where we focus our attention. When you focus on cultivating your inner prosperity, more good things will come your way! A prosperous and successful person is one whose heart is filled with inner prosperity and spiritual cultivation: someone whose words, thoughts, and deeds reflect joy, appreciation, and alignment to their soul.

As you work to cultivate inner prosperity, think of all of your accomplishments, even the small ones. Keep a journal—you might look back to the "Celebrating Me!" journal from Chapter Three—and write down each day's little successes and triumphs. By doing this, you become more mindful, and you'll value yourself more. You'll be kinder to yourself, and you'll grow and evolve more and more as a person and as a professional.

GETTING IN "THANKFUL MODE"

Living in today's world, it can be difficult to remain positive and connected to the present moment. Often times, between our busy schedules, our quest for external happiness, and the flood of bad news and violence we see on TV and in movies every day, we are at risk of becoming more negative and disconnected from ourselves.

Sometimes, we focus on what we think is wrong, or what we're missing in our lives. We only choose to celebrate and feel grateful when something big happens: a wedding, a graduation, a promotion, etc. We have a tendency to forget that we need to appreciate and be thankful for the little things, too.

Gratitude is essential! If life had gone just a little differently, you might not have all that you do right now. Cultivating gratitude enables you to be in the moment. Every day, focus on your blessings and think of all the things you can be grateful for: your house (yes, you have a place to live! Some people don't have one), your health, your family, your car, your job, your business, your friends, your pet, nature, even your challenges—they help you grow and evolve.

The more grateful you are, the more good things will come your way. Remember, we get what we focus our attention on. It's your choice as to whether you focus on the negative or on the positive. So make a conscious choice to focus on the positive: I can guarantee that you'll begin to create little miracles in your life.

Appreciating the beauty in little things as well as expressing gratitude for the wonderful things you already have makes life easier and more pleasant not only for you, but also for those around you.

When you are in that "thankful mode," your light is brighter. Therefore, you will attract more people and more situations that are on the same vibrational level as you. Gratitude is that powerful! It can turn the negative into the positive, and it can transform our feelings of fear into expansive feelings like love and joy in just a second. Being thankful leads us to growth and plants the seeds for attracting magical things into our lives.

If you want to feel happier and healthier (physically and emotionally), gratitude is a key quality to cultivate daily. Having a grateful attitude towards life expands our consciousness: we feel we can achieve what we set out to do, and are filled with optimism and hope.

Taking the perspective of gratitude allows us to notice more and more gifts and experiences we can feel grateful for. Gratitude allows us to focus on the real, which is essential to achieving anything we want. It puts us in touch with the Divine—the source of all creation—and in turn, all that we need becomes available to us.

Here's an exercise that includes various ways to focus on gratitude throughout the day.

1. Write down five things that you're grateful for each morning and night before you go to bed.

2. Journal based on the following prompts every day:

   - How can I express gratitude and appreciation to others today?

   - What am I grateful for about myself today?

DEEPENING YOUR SPIRITUAL CONNECTION

Each day, we are exposed to information and external issues that have the power to trigger conditioned behaviors and beliefs. We might experience this when dealing with difficult family members or coworkers, or receiving messages from society, our culture, or the media. We are constantly bombarded with information and demands that we measure up to certain pre-established standards.

As I said before, if we are not mindful, we tend to base our self-worth on external factors like material things, accomplishments, approval from people, etc. Even though it may seem that this is part of being human and living in this world and era, it can be very exhausting and draining. It creates an internal struggle, and our ego-mind gets louder, often leading us to feel anxious and even depressed.

Some people think they find comfort in their numbness without even realizing that they're using certain addictive behaviors to fill the void. Because they are afraid to look deeper, some people use food, drugs, alcohol, cigarettes, retail therapy, the internet, social media, sex, gambling, exercise, or TV to avoid their feelings. Some register for different coaching programs, classes, and/or certification programs at the same time to keep themselves busy, or in the hopes that these programs will solve their confusion and challenges.

Studying and trying to better ourselves is never bad. However, when you begin with the belief that this will be the solution to your lack of fulfillment and unhappiness, you'll realize that at the end of the day you've spent money with no real results. When we believe answers will come from the outside, these attempts are just a means to escape and keep ourselves busy while we wait for happiness to come. Our lives are predominantly outward-oriented. However, the source of joy, answers, and all our potential actually comes from within.

We are spiritual beings having a human experience, but with so many external demands, we tend to ignore our spiritual connection and growth. So what can we do to stay grounded and more connected to our authentic selves?

We have to accept who we really are: we are whole, complete, lovable, and worthy beings—the way we are *now*. Sure, there's always room for growth and improvement, but we are already perfect the way we are.

I'd like to pass on some advice shared by many of my mentors and teachers: we need to develop sacred, non-negotiable, and unapologetic daily rituals that allow us to re-connect with the Divine and with our souls. This is our quiet time, our time just to be with ourselves, and it is so beneficial for many areas of our lives.

To strengthen our inner connection and develop spiritually, we need to set aside a few minutes each day; I suggest a minimum of twenty to thirty minutes. Taking this time in the morning, before you begin your routine, is ideal: that way, you start the day by grounding yourself and setting intentions. You might also enjoy a ritual at the end of the day to stop and reflect.

Activities you can include during this time are: journaling, praying, expressing gratitude, meditating, picking an Angel card, reading/listening to something inspirational, doing yoga, going out for a walk in nature, drawing, coloring a mandala, etc. You might light incense or candles or diffuse essential oils to create a more relaxing and cozy setting.

Make your daily practice as peaceful, creative, or stimulating as you please. Whatever you choose to do, do it consistently and mindfully. When you are fully present, you can feel the joy of connecting at a deeper level with your soul and listening to the messages it shares with you. This is the key to finding the answers you need.

Something else that I consider important in this daily practice is following my intuition. We need to listen and trust our inner wisdom. Trust that you are not your conditions; you're not your struggles. Listen to your intuition and trust yourself.

Intuition—what some call your inner voice or Divine inner guidance—is a spiritual gift that we all have. But, unfortunately, a lot of us live our lives using only the five senses that are familiar to us. We neglect the reconnection to the most powerful sense that we all were born with.

I once read that Gandhi called this voice "the voice of truth." He said that this voice is as loud as our willingness to listen. There is no such thing as someone with no intuition: everyone possesses this extraordinary gift. It is a mental muscle, and like all muscles, it must be exercised so that we can activate it at full capacity and make it stronger.

Listening to our intuition is a skill that has to be worked at and developed. Although we all have intuition, we do not always pay attention to it. Just know that when you're faced with an important decision in your personal or professional life, you can look inside for an inspired insight. Trust that it will guide you in the right direction.

In order to listen to our intuition, we have to work on being grounded and connected to our heart first. Only then are our minds quiet enough for us to listen to our inner guidance. When we learn to quiet the constant external noise, our negative voices, and the busyness that we face in life every day, we open up a channel that allows us to listen to our intuition and follow our Divine inner guidance. And when we do follow our inner voices, we are in-flow with life; we live lives that are more authentic, and full of meaning, love, joy, connection and freedom.

I invite you to make a commitment to give your inner voice your full attention and allow it to become stronger for the next 30 days. To do so, just fill in your name and sign the commitment below:

I, _____, will allow myself to trust and follow my inner voice, my Divine inner guidance, or my "gut feeling"—that intuitive side of my being that is perfect and all-knowing. I will suspend my need to know exactly why, and begin to explore and experience this spiritual gift.

Signature _____

Date _____

Remember, having a daily spiritual ritual practice, combined with a healthy diet and lifestyle, will contribute to your general well-being and will allow you to connect with your authentic self and a more expansive energy and higher vibration for longer periods of time.

CONNECTING WITH YOUR INNER JOY

Joy is a crucial subject because I know a lot of people struggle with this every day. I've been there myself, so I know how painful it can be. We only have to look around ourselves to see how common this is: we may even have people close to us, like family members or close friends, struggling on a daily basis. This can also affect us in different ways.

I've noticed that some people have been disconnected from joy for so long that they have nearly forgotten how to feel joyful. Some people only connect with that feeling when something big happens in their life—a celebration, the birth of a child, etc. The truth is that we all need to focus on joy by clearing away the barriers to it. Most importantly, we must practice getting comfortable with joy.

It is key to work on this, because the core of all healing, wellbeing, and even success and abundance is based on aligning ourselves with the higher vibrational energy we create when we connect with our inner joy. And who doesn't want to be joyful? We ALL want to feel more joy, but joy is still so elusive to so many people.

When we were kids, our connection to joy felt very natural and easy because it is our natural state. We are spiritual beings, and our true nature is happiness, joy, and freedom. If you doubt this, all you have to do is spend some time with a little kid to see it clearly. They're always playing and laughing; they're spontaneous, creative, curious, lighthearted, free, and cheerful. It's natural for them to be in that state because it is the core of their being.

That's how we were too, but with the years, we have disconnected from that state. We became distant from the real *us*, as if our real selves went into hiding. We ended up living from our conditioned parts, behaviors, and stories. That's actually when our disconnection to joy began.

Joy is the key to easily finding solutions to our challenging problems, having better relationships, and getting closer to our sweetest dreams. When we feel joy, we're living from a higher vibration, and we are open to seeing opportunities that are hidden when we go through life with feelings and emotions that put us on a lower vibration or fill us with negative energy.

156

Here's the secret: whether this moment is joyful or not depends on our perspective. The moment will not make us joyful; we ourselves make the moment joyful. With mindfulness and awareness, we can make of any moment a joyful moment. Joy is an art, because we can create whatever we can from any situation or circumstance.

Being joyful is a conscious choice we make as to how we show up in life every day, in every single moment in our personal and professional lives. Joy is not a place that you get to when you retire, your kids go to college, you pay off debt, you find a new job, you find your ideal partner, etc. There is really no place to arrive. Our life is a series of conscious choices, and it's intended to be a consistent process of growth and expansion. The Universe or the Divine is always giving us the opportunity to expand and be joyful every single minute of the day. Sadly, we're not open to seeing the possibilities.

When we expect external things to bring us joy, we live lives that are not aligned with the truth of our souls: we're not living life *on purpose*. We're not taking the time to connect with ourselves, or to love and value ourselves for who we really are. We all have a hidden reservoir of limitless sacred power and energy; it is available, and waiting for us to connect and align to it so that we can see miracles unfold in our lives.

However, we tend to control how we want things to be: our ego-minds drive the bus. We tell ourselves, "If I get there, then that's when I'll be happy..." The truth is that every moment is meant to be lived joyfully—*no matter what*. We always have the choice, and we always create our lives based on our decisions and choices.

One of the biggest mistakes that people make is believing that other people and external circumstances are responsible for their joy. When we hold this belief, we give our power away. We need to embrace the reality that our joy is in our own hands every minute of the day. We are the ones making that choice every day. Joy is a choice, not a result.

We have lived in a fear-based society since we were kids, and all throughout our lives we've been conditioned—from our families to our culture—with thoughts, choices and actions that are based in fear. When we experience fear of failure, getting sick, death, poverty, pain, loss, loneliness, or separation, we forgot about our own divinity. We lose sight of the reality that we are part of a Divine tapestry that connects us all through unconditional love, and we forget how powerful we are when it comes to creating the lives we want.

The truth is that the more fearful we are, the more we try to control our lives, circumstances, and others around us. This makes us go against the flow of life and what's natural for us—love and joy. In turn, we give away our power and we feel a sense of struggle and separation.

We were never taught to connect inwardly, which is why everything is conditioned to external things. However, the solution truly lies in going inwards to seek answers. When we expect external things to change what's going on inside, we embrace an illusion. External things will only help to avoid the reality of what's going on inside, and will make us place responsibility on the wrong factors.

Remember, we only live authentically if we leave the victim role behind us and step into our power, becoming the architects of our own fates. The search must be done internally. You cannot change something you are not aware of. We will experience in the outside world the chaos and disorder of our inner world; that, my friend, is what you will continue to attract if you do not put some order in your inner world first and choose to start connecting with your soul and your inner joy.

Our joy is the consequence of the thoughts we choose to have, what we focus on, how we treat ourselves moment by moment, and the choices that we make. The power is always in the present moment. It might not be easy sometimes, but it's time to step into your inner joy on a more consistent basis.

So how do we reconnect with our natural state and feel joy every day? How do we begin to feel that we are whole and enough, no matter what our circumstances are? We simply need to start living our lives from our authentic selves. We need to shift our perspective from ego to Spirit. They way to start is by having an unapologetic ritual every day, and by being consistent, as I mentioned above.

We have to leave our fears, insecurities, and confusion behind, and we have to let go of the need to control: these things make us live constricted lives. Instead, we can let our souls guide us through life with ease. We do this by connecting with ourselves every day, listening to our inner wisdom, and trusting that our True Selves are wise enough to live with ease, expansiveness, and joy. To cultivate joy in our lives, we need to shift from the limitations of our ego to the freedom of our Spirit.

QUESTIONS TO PONDER

Feeling joyful is a conscious choice that you need to make over and over again so that your old conditioning and agreements don't get in the way.

- When you think of joy, what feelings and memories come up for you?

- How often do you feel joy in your life? How often do you *want* to feel joy?

- What are some ways in which you can commit to connecting to your inner joy on a daily basis?

CHAPTER *Nine*

Living Your Awakened Life

Living Your Awakened Life

*W*hen you discover who you really are, you awaken to life. The tools introduced in Chapters One through Eight help you move towards that discovery—and this is just the beginning. You've already made huge progress by reading this book. However, you will discover that it takes work to stay awake. The first step is awareness, because without awareness we have no choices available to us. The next step is to go from being aware to leading a fully awakened life. This is something that we need to keep consciously and intentionally choosing every moment of our lives.

I'm sure you know very well by now that living out of alignment with who you truly are will result in a life of struggle, imbalance, and unhappiness. When we live life on autopilot, usually, the decisions that we make come from a place of fear; they are not aligned with the truths of our souls. Therefore, we fall into an endless cycle of stuckness which brings significant pain.

We come to this beautiful planet with the mission to grow, evolve, and experience joy. We are all the same, and we are in this stunning world to learn, serve, teach, and love—to become better versions of ourselves. We all seek these things in one way or another. Moreover, the greatest responsibility we have while we are inhabiting this wonderful planet is towards *ourselves*.

Remember what I said in the introduction? Nobody will come to save you. You are responsible for your own life. When we live in alignment with our True Selves, we help raise the level of collective consciousness, we make the world a better place.

The human being is the only species of all living beings on Earth that is fully aware of the existence of other species—not to mention beings living in other countries and other cultures. That's what makes us different, and a superior species; we have a higher consciousness. But what I've seen time and time again is that not everyone appreciates the miracle and gift of living on this beautiful, rich, and diverse planet.

My hope is that the tools in this book have helped you to understand that if we all sought within ourselves—if we all aimed to truly know ourselves, to grow and transform our consciousness— there would be a lot less violence in the world. What would happen if we were all grateful for the good things we have? If we felt that the core of our whole beings was love and joy? For starters, we would have more respect for other living beings on Earth. We would not manipulate or control others, nor would we project our fears, limiting beliefs, or judgments onto others.

At this point, I'm sure you see that we cannot continue living on autopilot. It doesn't serve us when we blame others or our circumstances for our unhappiness. Rather, it is our responsibility to act in service of living bigger and fuller lives. Now is the time to take our own personal power back and start becoming more aware, more alive, and therefore more awakened.

At the end of the day, it's all about commitment. Like Iyanla Vanzant said, "When you make a decision and a commitment to do something good for yourself, it is like dropping a pebble in a pond. It has a rippling effect. The firmer the decision, the stronger the frequency and wider the range of things that will be reached."

THE ONGOING PRACTICE OF SELF-FULFILLMENT

It has taken me years of practice and determination to become more self-aware. And I'm still a work in progress; we all are. It takes years of practice to undo habits that have been ingrained in us for decades. Furthermore, it takes commitment, determination, and radical self-love to choose consistency. It is difficult to stop living at the mercy of our egos. In fact, I still have days where I find myself navigating in the rough and negative waters of my own mind, and falling into old stories that I know are not serving me anymore. However, after consistent practice, I find it now takes me much less time to become aware and shift myself into alignment again.

It's been an intense and beautiful journey. I love experiencing awe for the little things, the tiny magical blessings that I get to witness every day: I let myself be mesmerized by sunrises, sunsets, and the beauty of a tree or a flower. I feel joy as I witness a dragonfly or a butterfly flutter close to me. All it takes to stand in awe of the little things is awareness and an open mind. When we start to see the beauty that surrounds us every day, we let life surprise us in the most unexpected ways.

We can choose to be inspired, or we can choose to focus on what isn't working: at the end of the day it's up to us. I've learned the hard way that we get what we focus on, so I've committed to focusing on the miracles of this adventure called life. I allow myself to dream and to take action towards my dreams, even if it's one baby step at a time. It is, for all of us, safe and healthy to dream; it doesn't matter how old we are.

I keep reminding myself that I am worthy of my desires. I unapologetically tune into what my heart tells me, and I believe in my gifts. I keep committing to my True Self over and over again so that I don't fall back into old patterns. I make sure that I have fun exploring my gifts, and that I pay attention to what fills my heart with joy, and most importantly, that I take inspired action.

When we listen to our inner voices, we learn which activities and pursuits will bring us joy and a sense of fulfillment. For me, this means going to voice classes: singing makes my soul so happy, so why would I deny it? I also attend painting classes where I explore my creativity. As of writing this, I am listening to the whispers of my soul, and hearing that my next step is to sign up for piano classes. I have always loved music so much. In fact, it's actually what motivated me to learn English: I wanted to understand the lyrics of the music I loved when I was a kid. Some of these activities may resonate with you, but I encourage you to tune in to your own True Self for inspiration on what will help you feel light, joyful, and free.

I'm committed to living a life of true fulfillment. Even when I feel fear, I take inspired action. Each day, I make the choice to stay aware and awake, and to take steps towards my dreams so that I can continue becoming a better version of myself. This is the ultimate purpose for all of us: to start with ourselves, and from there, to spread more joy and make a positive impact on the planet.

FEAR AS A SUPERPOWER TO FUEL COURAGE

Fear will show up almost every time you decide to do something new, so how can you move through your fears and continue to live an awakened life? If you haven't already asked yourself this question— or even if you have—you can use it as a journaling prompt.

As humans, we will experience fear many times in our lives. We're wired to feel fear because we're built for survival, and fear is the primal instinct that keeps us safe. But when real fear is not present—there is no tiger jumping towards us, our lives are not in danger—fear is almost never a good advisor. Fear distorts our perception and our decision-making process. The false fear trap can manifest in many subtle and confusing ways, but however it shows up, it prevents us from living lives that are authentic, fully expressed, and open to the depth of everything that's possible.

If fear holds you back from having the relationships, the financial success, the vitality, and the joyful, meaningful life you are meant to have, you're not alone, this is very common. The problem is that we tend to take the easy way out and stick to what's known and "safe" to us. Stepping out of our comfort zones and trying new things is very difficult because it triggers fears. We are afraid of the unknown, and we tend to cling to the comfort of what's uncomfortably well-known. However, as you already know, we can't reach happiness and fulfillment there.

You've come so far in this process already. By now, you have cultivated more awareness, so you know that it takes tremendous courage to face what we often want to ignore the most. Nonetheless, it is important to remind yourself that there will be no growth or change if you allow yourself to procrastinate or self-sabotage.

The truth is that no change can come from staying in the same place, making the same decisions, and taking the same risks. Once I really understood this, I was able to make a few difficult and scary decisions, but in the long run, these brought much growth, expansion, joy, and freedom into my life.

I love this quote from Abraham Maslow: "You will either step forward into Growth, or you will step back into Safety."

Even when you want to make positive changes in your life, fear will arise. You may wonder why fear arises even when you know a change is in alignment with your True Self. Years ago, I learned from one of my mentors the concept of "The Terror Barrier": the current paradigm or dynamic from which you operate in your daily life.

Imagine there is a square: everything that you know to be true in your world is contained within that box. I'm sure that at this point you understand that life is about evolving and expanding—and that we are often limited by our conditioned thoughts and patterns. Therefore, we tend to live within the limits of this square or this paradigm. When we begin to get clear on our dreams and life purpose, we begin to move closer to the edges of the square. (Typically, our dreams and visions are outside of the bounds of our paradigm.) At this point, your ego mind gets activated.

That is the Terror Barrier: the part of you that gives you a red alert signal. Because you're doing something unfamiliar that moves you towards the unknown, it wants to stop you. But, at this point of our work together, you understand that that's the ego mind's job: to stop you from taking risks.

Understanding this has been so helpful for me; when you want to make a big change and want to uplevel to the higher vibration that is in alignment with your dreams, the Terror Barrier can manifest. And misunderstanding the source of this sometimes intense feeling is what stops people in their tracks.

Keep in mind that fear is a normal part of the process of growth— it's not a signal to stop. The bigger the change, the bigger the fear. However, the more often that you leap, the more you get used to the discomfort and the process. At the end of the day, you know that we are always creating, either by default or design. I like design way better ... by default, you feel like a victim.

In order to thrive while you face changes or challenges in your life, you have to be willing to take different risks and intentionally step into growth so that you can get different results. Fear doesn't allow us to see possibilities: it limits our ability to see and move beyond the place in which our mind is stuck and what we see as possibilities.

With everything you've learned so far, you know that no matter how difficult we think the situation is, we must gather the courage to face it. We need to be brave while feeling afraid, and we need to reframe our relationship with fear. In fact, fear is healing: it will shine the light of awareness on what needs to change.

Here are a few techniques to help you move through fear:

1. *Name the fears as they come up.* Your protective ego wants to keep you safe at all cost: it does not like change, and it wants to keep you in your square. Many of your fears have no basis in reality; they feel real and big because you feed them by giving them energy and attention. Don't feed your fears by focusing on them. Instead, starve them by focusing on your next step.

2. *Breathe.* Our ego-minds are all about fear. Fear gets stuck in our bodies when we don't breathe. Notice that when you feel fear, your breathing is shallow. When anxiety and unease arise, take deep breaths into your belly, and try to move your body so that you can release them.

3. *Write your fears down on paper so that you can see them.* Which fears arise most frequently for you? Maybe you think to yourself, *I'm afraid that I'll fail, I'm not talented enough, I'll be judged, I won't be good enough, I won't make money,* or *I won't have enough.* How old do you feel when this fear comes up? A technique that I learned from one of my mentors, and worked wonders for me, is becoming aware of the age you were when this belief first arose. This can help you to shift into compassion for this younger or more vulnerable part of you. Then, you

169

can write out a response to the fear from the perspective of how old you are now. That will separate the younger and older parts of yourself and help you generate inner support so you can step out of that fear.

4. *Every day, write, "If I was not afraid, I would _____."* And fill in the blank. This helps you step out of your fears and work through them. Write a list of what you would do if you were not afraid. Every day, pick one item and do it. That way, you'll be practicing feeling fear and taking action anyway. The more you do this, the easier it gets. Start getting comfortable with the uncomfortable and move forward so that you can grow and expand.

When you lead an awakened life, fear feels like a path towards something richer because it invites expansion. Instead of feeling like a victim of it, see fear as a doorway: as you step through, you go beyond what's possible. Fear like nothing else can launch you forward in unimaginable ways, so see it as a friend trying to guide you to your freedom.

Here's the key: how someone chooses to perceive their fear is what makes *all* the difference in their life. I had a mentor tell me, "Those who choose to believe that the presence of fear represents proof of a flawed, weak character risk their dreams dying inside them."

I agree: denial and shame are dream killers. The more defensive thoughts we have, the more fear we will feel. We can't control everything that happens, and control is a key word here. We think giving in to fear will keep us safe. However, when we let fear control us, it becomes our worst enemy because it keeps us living small lives.

I personally have learned to dance with my sneaky and persistent fear almost every day of my life. Understanding the concept of the Terror Barrier and knowing that fear will be there always, fear and I became friends. In fact, I have fear to thank for so much in my life. Without it, you wouldn't be reading this book.

I truly appreciate my fear because it shines the light of awareness on what needs to be healed. I've learned to welcome its presence as evidence of my willingness to s-t-r-e-t-c-h beyond what's comfortable. Fear shows me another awesome opportunity to choose to believe that I am divinely loved and fully supported all the time.

We get very distressed about the unknown. However, uncertainty is the gateway to possibility. To use fear as fuel for courage, just feel curiosity and be open to the infinite possibilities that it holds. Fear is healing, transformative, and a catalyst for growth and expansion.

I've learned that being courageous is really about letting fear transform you, and for that, you have to come into the right relationship with uncertainty, make peace with impermanence, and wake up to who you really are. It means that you allow yourself to connect and align with your soul, despite what your conditioning is telling you. You have to ignore everything the voice of your ego-mind is screaming at you—it's just the Terror Barrier making its limits known.

When I was doing research about fear and courage, I came across the work of Dr. Lisa Rankin. According to her, data indicates that fear is a factor that predisposes us to disease. Fear could be argued to be as much of a health risk as a poor diet or smoking, and it gets confused with stress sometimes. Because again, fear lives deep in the shadows for most people. We try not to talk about it, yet we all struggle with it.

Fear can be a blessing, not only because it can protect you from danger, but also because it can wake you up. Fear points a finger at everything that needs to be healed in our lives. If you're brave enough to heal it, courage blossoms, and you'll find peace and freedom as the reward.

When you allow yourself to tap into your courage, you're simply allowing yourself to advance on your spiritual journey and to awaken to who you really are. Like any journey in life, this one requires time, practice, commitment, support, faith, and radical acts of self-compassion.

When you align with your True Self, the Universe increasingly draws into your life true joy, unconditional love, fulfillment, physical health, and a sense of freedom and connection with the Divine. You may lose your comfort zone, but what you'll gain when you commit to this journey is priceless. When you commit, you gain freedom like you've never had before.

So, are you willing to explore how courageous you really are? I want you to truly ponder this question.

WHO WOULD YOU BE IF FEAR WASN'T GETTING IN THE WAY?

What leaps of faith would you take? How would you feel if you woke up every day with nothing holding you back?

I can tell you from my own experience, and from what I've seen with my clients, that when you move past that Terror Barrier and into the realm of faith:

- You'll wake up excited about the endless possibilities ahead of you.

- You'll pay more attention to what you appreciate than what you lack.

- You won't feel the need to compromise your integrity in order to get approval.

- You'll be living from an authentic place, owning your story, and living life on your terms. Your life will not be based on "shoulds" anymore.

- You'll find that the work you do every day is filled with purpose and meaning.

- You'll navigate any lower vibrational feelings (fear, anxiety, anger, resentment, worry, disappointment) with more ease and be able to shift to higher vibrational feelings like love, joy, peace, and groundedness more quickly.

- You'll be amazed by what you're capable of—you'll tap into gifts that you were not aware you had.

- You'll get clarity about each step to take as you follow your path. Often, the steps won't be revealed until you commit to pursuing your path.

- Amazing synchronicities and coincidences will start to happen with more regularity in your life.

When you learn to work with fear rather than giving in to it, your relationships will improve in a magical way as you feel the joy and rightness of your path. You will relax and let others be who they are. You'll release the idea that other people need to be different for you to be happy. As you take the steps you need to be truly happy, you will experience a sense of deeper connection.

When you stop living in fear, you provide an amazing example to those around you. You show them that it's possible to live being true to yourself. This will have a positive impact on your kids, too. I invite you to ask yourself this question that I read once, from Brené Brown: "Are you the adult that you want your child to grow up to be?" And remember, your dreams are as hungry as your fears, so make sure you're feeding your dreams and starving your fears!

173

REDEFINING SUCCESS

When you have awakened your True Self and are living life from that place, you start seeing success through another lens. You now see that success starts when you have clarity on what you want, what you stand for, and when you're living your life with courage and authenticity. Success means achieving *your* own goals, not anyone else's.

You know that success is not measured by the material possessions we have or how far up we are on the managerial ladder. You recognize that success comes when we live life on our own terms, when we know what we want and we love what we do—when we create our lives from a place of conscious awareness, self-love, and responsibility.

We all tend to get stuck on a hamster wheel at some point in our lives. Sometimes, we do things that aren't good for us and stay in situations in which we shouldn't, all in the name of comfort and "safety." But only a few that are leading awakened lives will take action to start making positive changes in spite of the fears that may get triggered.

Here are some of the things that awakened people will do consistently as they work towards their definition of success:

- *They don't quit.* They know that perseverance is key and that many times, when they feel like quitting, they're actually almost there. They focus on the lessons learned to improve. They always keep in mind why they started, and then push onward. Their "why" and their Vision are their driving force.

- *They don't see themselves as victims.* Awakened, successful people know that they are the creators of their own reality. They make choices instead of excuses. They are accountable for their own life, career, relationships, health, etc.

- *They are action-takers.* They don't believe in "someday" or leaving things on the back burner. They set goals and take bold actions towards their visions, because they know this will bring growth, expansion, and fulfillment in their lives.

- *They don't resist change.* Successful and awakened people are flexible; they go with the flow and embrace change knowing that there's always a lesson and a hidden treasure.

- *They are aware of their worth.* They value and appreciate themselves. They're aware of their uniqueness, the value that they bring to the table, and the impact their gifts will make in the world.

- *They honor themselves.* They are clear on their core values, gifts, and mission, and they have well-defined boundaries—but it doesn't mean that they only think of themselves.

- *They invest in themselves.* They know that investing money, time and energy on their growth will pay off for themselves and those around them. Successful and awakened people don't make excuses and don't put other people's needs ahead of theirs—they know they are worth it!

Successful and awakened people are curious, creative, respectful, competent, and persistent. They know that the results they get are in proportion to their commitment and the effort they put in.

One of the biggest fears that might hold us back is fear of failure. We have been conditioned to be afraid of failure, and a lot of people see it as something to be ashamed of. However, as I've said before, you can only be successful if you do things in a different way, and if you take different risks. When you truly live an awakened life, you will be firm in your commitment to stepping out of your comfort zone and going past the Terror Barrier!

There are so many lessons to be learned from failure, but you will not give yourself the chance to grow if you keep yourself safe in what's known and secure. When it comes to overcoming your fear of failure, revisit this list of what successful and awakened people do consistently. In addition:

- *Adopt a "Growth Mindset."* See failure as part of success. Know that every experience is a learning experience that will make you stronger and will help you grow. Always ask yourself these powerful questions when you feel that you have failed:

  - What worked?

  - What didn't work?

  - What can I improve next time?

  - What is at least one gift from this situation?

- *Become aware of your personal story.* When we get very upset and beat ourselves up for failing at something, we need to be mindful that there might be a core belief underneath that needs to be brought to the surface. One that is very common is "I am not enough" or "I am not good enough." Always explore from a place of curiosity and being gentle with yourself. Once you discover what the story is, commit to changing it to a more positive and supportive one.

One of the keys to overcoming your fear of failure is to have a positive and optimistic attitude. Thinking positively will not only help you to feel more confident, but will also help you to see the gifts in every situation. In addition, when you feel fear, revisit your vision and what you want to do. Then, go back to your "Why." This will give you the kick in the butt you need to take action!

I'm sure you know that your biggest fear should not be failure: rather, it should be staying stuck and living a small life filled with self-imposed limitations. When you don't take the risk of failure, you keep yourself from living a life that is an authentic expression of your true desires and calling.

One last thing: *Please* stop hiding who you are, stop hiding your greatness! If you're not allowing yourself to be who you were created to be, you're doing a disservice to your unique mission here on the planet and you're dishonoring your Creator. You have an important role in the world at this time. Dream big and push through your self-imposed limitations so that others can see your shining light and feel inspired to give themselves permission to do the same. We need more awakened life in this world.

Give yourself permission to start a new story today! Life is a magical gift, so allow yourself to create a happier, healthier, more joyful, and more purposeful story. You deserve all the happiness in the world. Living life authentically and *on purpose* is your birthright, and when you truly claim that right, you live an awakened life!

I'm honored and thrilled that you choose to give yourself permission to awaken to life.

Love and Blessings,
Patricia

Acknowledgments

I feel so much gratitude for the many wonderful people, including mentors, friends and family members, who have inspired and supported me through this journey, and have been so instrumental in making this dream a reality.

I would like to specially thank:

My loving parents, for whom I am so grateful. You are the best parents I could have ever asked for. Without you, I wouldn't be who I am today. I love you with all my heart!

My sister, for being one of my best friends even in the distance.

My nieces, two beautiful beams of light who are full of potential to make a difference in this world.

My dear husband! You are the best thing that has happened to me. Thanks for believing in me and supporting me along this journey, even when I have doubted myself.

Linda Joy, my loving publisher, whose trust in me made such a difference in how I saw myself as a writer, and in how I shared my truth. Your support has made the birthing of this book possible.

Bryna Haynes, whose magical and loving editorial support has been instrumental to sharing this work in my authentic voice.

All my clients, who inspired me to develop this material.

All my friends who, in one way or another, have been there for me all these years.

Two very special souls (Anna and Yelen) who went home too soon, but who were certainly the catalyst for my own awakening and this book becoming a reality.

Shelley Riutta, for holding my hand at the beginning of this journey of self-discovery. Thank you for believing in me when I couldn't believe in myself, and for lovingly supporting me when fears and overwhelming emotions were showing up in so many sneaky ways. You made such a difference in my life!

And finally, *you,* reader. It makes my soul so happy to know that you're allowing yourself to go inward and giving yourself permission to explore this beautiful journey of awakening to life. You and I, and all the people that we'll touch with the ripple of goodness we create in this process, are contributing to the creation of a more awakened and loving planet.

Helpful Resources

*B*elow is a list of some of the mentors and inspirational teachers I've been studying and following for years, and whose teachings have shaped my message and work here on the planet. You may find their words and their work valuable as well.

Jesus	Buddha
Osho	Krishnamurti
Friedrich Nietzsche	The Dalai Lama
Deepak Chopra	Thich Nhat Hanh
Carl Jung	Carl Rogers
Abraham Maslow	Eckhart Tolle
Dr. Wayne Dyer	Louise Hay
Marianne Williamson	Bob Proctor
Mary Morrissey	Brené Brown
Tony Robbins	Steve Maraboli
Jack Canfield	Gay Hendricks
Byron Katie	Dr. Margaret Paul
Dr. Elaine N. Aron	Esther and Jerry Hicks
Rhonda Byrne	Daniel Goleman
Alan Cohen	Don Miguel Ruiz
Napoleon Hill	Florence Scovel Shinn
Wallace D. Wattles	James Allen
Price Pritchett	John Randolph Price
Orison Marden	Jim Rohn
Zig Ziglar	Helen Schucman/ACIM

About *Patricia*

PATRICIA YOUNG is a Transformational Life Coach and Strategist, international best-selling author, the host of the popular Awakening to Life podcast, the founder of Inner Prosperity Academy, and the author of the upcoming book, *Awakening to Life: Your Sacred Guide to Creating a Life of Purpose, Magic, and Miracles* (Inspired Living Publishing). She is a frequent contributor to *Aspire Magazine* and a sought-after media and summit guest.

Patricia passionately supports sensitive and growth-oriented women in identifying and living their highest life vision. Her keen insight, nurturing energy, and proven strategies help women take action to bring this vision into reality so they can live the life they came here to live—both personally and professionally.

Visit www.InnerProsperityAcademy.com to learn more about Patricia's offerings, and for empowering and supportive content.

About The Publisher

*F*ounded in 2010 by Inspirational Catalyst, radio show host, and *Aspire Magazine* Publisher Linda Joy, Inspired Living Publishing (ILP) is an international best-selling inspirational boutique publishing company dedicated to spreading a message of love, positivity, feminine wisdom, and self-empowerment to women of all ages, backgrounds, and life paths. Linda's multimedia brands reach over 44,000 subscribers and a social media community of over 24,000 women.

Through our highly-successful anthology division, we have brought ten books and over 300 visionary female authors to best-seller status. Our powerful, high-visibility publishing, marketing, and list-building packages have brought these authors—all visionary entrepreneurs, coaches, therapists, and health practitioners—the positive, dynamic exposure they need to attract their ideal audience and thrive in their businesses.

Inspired Living Publishing also publishes single-author books by visionary female authors whose messages are aligned with Linda's philosophy of authenticity, empowerment, and personal transformation. Recent best-selling releases include the award-winning *Being Love: How Loving Yourself Creates Ripples of Transformation in Your Relationships and the World*, by Dr. Debra L. Reble; and the multiple-award-winning *The Art of Inspiration: An Editor's Guide to Writing Powerful, Effective Inspirational & Personal Development Books*, by ILP Chief Editor Bryna René Haynes.

ILP's family of authors reap the benefits of being a part of a sacred family of inspirational multimedia brands which deliver the best in transformational and empowering content across a wide range of platforms. Our hybrid publishing packages and *à la carte* marketing and media packages provide visionary female authors with access to our proven best-seller model and high-profile multimedia exposure across all of Linda's imprints (including *Aspire Magazine*, the "Inspired Conversations" radio show on OMTimes Radio, the Inspired Living Giveaway, Inspired Living Secrets, and exposure to Linda's loyal personal audience of over 44,000 women).

If you're ready to publish your transformational book, or share your story in one of ours, we invite you to join us! Learn more about our publishing services at www.InspiredLivingPublishing.com.

Made in the USA
Middletown, DE
24 March 2018